Spiritual Guidelines
for Souls Seeking God

Fr. Basil W. Maturin

Spiritual Guidelines
for
Souls Seeking God

SOPHIA INSTITUTE PRESS
Manchester, New Hampshire

Sophia Institute Press
Box 5284, Manchester, NH 03108
1-800-888-9344

www.SophiaInstitute.com

Sophia Institute Press® is a registered trademark of Sophia Institute.

Library of Congress Cataloging-in-Publication Data

Names: Maturin, B. W. (Basil William), 1847-1915, author.
Title: Spiritual guidelines for souls seeking God / Fr. Basil W. Maturin.
Other titles: Some principles and practices of the spiritual life
Description: Manchester, New Hampshire : Sophia Institute Press, 2017. |
  Originally published under title: Some principles and practices of the
  spiritual life : London : Longmans, Green, 1896.
Identifiers: LCCN 2016046608 | ISBN 9781622823581 (pbk. : alk. paper)
Subjects: LCSH: Spiritual life. | Spiritual life—Catholic Church. |
  Beatitudes. | Virtues.
Classification: LCC BV4501.3 .M2885 2017 | DDC 248.4/82—dc23 LC record
available at https://lccn.loc.gov/2016046608

First printing

Contents

☙

Spiritual Guidelines
for Souls Seeking God

Chapter 1

Cultivate the Virtues
That Underlie Holiness

Besides the general effort that every Christian must make to do what is right and to keep from what is wrong, it is important that he should have some special and definite aim that will help to keep him from dissipating his strength.

The end of the Christian life is, of course, *holiness*, but holiness is rather an indefinite thing to beginners, and it may manifest itself in many forms. And those who would attain to holiness must begin as they are, with their many sins and imperfections and ignorances, and work toward an end that becomes clearer as they advance and yet ever more difficult of attainment.

Indeed, they have to work toward an end that at first they cannot see, for only as the eye of the soul becomes purified does it get to see clearly what holiness means and how imperfect were its first conceptions of it.

It is a good thing, therefore, to concentrate our efforts, to be definite in our aim, to set before ourselves clearly some one purpose, some special virtue to strive after, on the attainment of which we shall have advanced considerably toward holiness of life.

Now, there are two kinds of virtues that we may seek. First, there are particular virtues that may counteract certain specific evil tendencies of the soul and help to overcome individual sins. The acquirement of these virtues is, of course, essential to the advancement of all. One may need to conquer sloth by diligence, or pride by humility, or irritability by patience; but this does not necessarily lead the soul to its end; it needs more than this. One may overcome certain individual sins and never go further or even aim at holiness.

There are, therefore, other more comprehensive virtues that involve in their acquisition much more than merely any one virtue or grace and that lead on definitely and directly to holiness of life. Such virtues cannot be gained, in any degree, without a very manifest growth in holiness; for they attack not merely one sin but the root of all the sin that is in us. In proportion as we acquire them, sin loses its hold upon our whole system: its vigor flags. The old man loses strength because the new man grows stronger; the sun rises over the whole being, the ice-bound nature thaws, and all the seeds of the new life begin to bud and blossom.

There are some people who seem never to get beyond the attack on individual sins and the aim after particular virtues. They do not get a large and comprehensive view of the ailments of their nature or perceive in what its perfection consists: they attack, so to speak, each separate symptom of their disease but they have never made a diagnosis of their state and attacked that which is the cause of all these different symptoms. They resemble the man in the Gospel who asked our Lord, "Which is the greatest commandment in the law?"[1] as though each commandment stood separate and disconnected from all the others,

---

[1] Matt. 22:36.

and as if a person might set himself to keep one perfectly to the neglect of all the others.

The observance of the Law as a whole seems scarcely to have occurred to him as a possibility, for he did not perceive that the details of the Decalogue were the expression in various relations of one great and comprehensive principle.

So our Lord answers him by showing him that the only way to observe them was by striving after the principle that underlay them all. He says: "You will never be able to keep the commandments if your aim is to observe them one by one. The spirit that underlies them all is love; strive after that, and you will find that in proportion as you gain that all-embracing virtue, you are observing all the commandments."

So, on the other hand, St. James says, "Whosoever shall keep the whole law, and yet offend in one point, he is guilty of all";[2] that is to say, by the deliberate violation of one of the commandments, one shows himself in antagonism to the spirit and principle of the moral law.

Our aim, therefore, should be to strive after those more comprehensive virtues that involve the spirit of holiness and bring in their train a multitude of graces, although this will, of course, necessitate the constant wrestling with individual sins. But it involves more: it involves a positive rather than a negative life. Its method is to aim at a spirit that necessarily protects one from sin.

We do not wish to develop a merely colorless character of which it can be said that it does not display any marked or definite faults. We want to develop a character, on the contrary, that is marked and definite; that shines with bright virtues; that puts itself forth in action, strong and vigorous. We have not in any

[2] James 2:10.

way got near a definition of God when we say He is not unjust, or cruel, or evil.

God is love and holiness.

And it is the same with man: he is not to be content with eliminating, one after another, those evident faults that disfigure his character. He has done nothing toward a holy life until his character can be defined in positive rather than in negative terms; in stating what he *is* rather than what he *is not*. The wise physician sets himself, not merely to cure one ailment or another but to build up the constitution with a vigorous health, strong enough to resist the attacks of disease.

And the soul will do this by building up its spiritual life on principles that undermine all the evil that is in it by developing such virtues that bring it face-to-face with God, such virtues that strike at the root of sin.

It is possible to set oneself to fight against his sins and in the struggle never to get out of himself, never to get really nearer to God. It is possible, perhaps more than possible; for the method of struggle sometimes seems to keep people down rather than raise them up.

What a difference there is in the whole character and religious bearing between one whose struggle consists merely in an effort not to give in to any sharp speech and uncharitableness and one who, with the same fault, sets himself with all his might to gain the love of God and the love of others in and for God. Such a person aims at something vastly higher than the mere victory over his sin; and even in his failures on the way, we feel that he has far outstripped his companion, who may not fail so badly but has not aimed so high. The one, when he has overcome his fault, may still be no nearer to positive love; the other is on the way to it long before his fault is overcome.

Now, this is the underlying principle of our Lord's teaching. He begins His teaching with the Beatitudes. In these He lays down the great laws of the life of holiness. They are given, not like the old law, in the form of prohibitions — "Thou shalt not" — but in the form of blessings. It is not "Cursed are the fornicators and adulterers" but "Blessed are the pure in heart."[3]

This may seem but another way of stating the same truth but we shall see that it is not; it is the expression of a great principle. The new law does not merely forbid men to do what is positively wrong; it begins a step higher than that; it takes us into that loftier region in which we are to be set free from the mere curb of prohibitions by living under the blessings of active obedience.

The old law forbade positive impurity: "Thou shalt not commit adultery."[4] The new law turns away from the sin and directs the soul to God: "Blessed are the pure in heart: for they shall see God."[5] In that vision of God to which this beatitude points the soul, there is no need to warn against such sin; the soul is freed from it; it is striving after that which makes it impossible.

Again, the old law said, "Thou shalt not bear false witness,"[6] and those who live in its spirit may strive very hard not to slander others. The new law begins on a higher level: it bids men aim at that which makes slander impossible: "Blessed are the peacemakers: for they shall be called the children of God."[7] It says: Do not be content with being in the world negatively, doing no

---

3 Matt. 5:8.
4 Exod. 20:14.
5 Matt. 5:8.
6 Exod. 20:16.
7 Matt. 5:9.

harm to others; try positively to do good, to make peace, and this as a child of God.

The old law forbade covetousness and stealing; the new turns the whole bent of the soul in another direction; away from the things of earth to the things of heaven: "Blessed are the poor in spirit: for theirs is the kingdom of heaven."[8]

One might keep the letter of the eighth and tenth commandments all one's life and never attain to the spirit of the first beatitude. No one could strive after the spirit of this beatitude without being set free, more than free, from all that these commandments prohibit.

Living under the principle of the law of prohibitions, one might obey the letter and never develop a character enlarged and enriched by positive and active goodness. One might, as it were, stand on the borderland between right and wrong, not doing positive wrong, and that is all, keeping his nature under bit and bridle from breaking away into a life of sin, ever conscious of a power of evil within that is ready to assert itself if the rein is loosened.

Under the principle of the new law, such a state of things is impossible: the soul is not content with restraints; it has passed into the region of its true development; it has been shown, not what it is *not* to do, but what it is *to do*; and the line of its development is in direct opposition to that in which its danger lies.

This, then, is the principle of the Christian life: it is positive rather than negative; it aims at something very much higher than keeping from definite acts of sin; it looks upon all laws of constraint as useless unless they tend to direct the currents of life

---

[8] Matt. 5:3.

toward their true end. It does not look upon such laws as ends in themselves, nor does it consider that by the mere submitting to the letter of such laws the soul has fulfilled their purpose.

No; habits of honesty, habits of prayer are mere bondage unless they are helping somehow the production of a free, honest, and prayerful nature. The only object in bandaging and twisting a man's crooked leg is that someday it may get a straightness into it that will make it keep its true shape when it is set free from bandages. If that day is never coming, bandaging is mere wanton cruelty. Better take the bandages off and let it be crooked, if it is getting no inner straightness and will be crooked as soon as they are removed.

So all these commandments and prohibitions that God lays before us: they are mere cruelty; they merely torture and worry humanity; they come to nothing unless within them some free law of inner rectitude is growing. One looks across God's great moral hospital, sees crooked souls tied up in constraint, and wonders—as one might who looked through a surgeon's ward—behind how many of those bandages an inner life is gathering that someday will ask no binding up and need nothing but its own liberty to be its law.

It is a strange question. Suppose tomorrow all the laws of constraint should be repealed together; all social penalties, all public restrictions, lifted off together; nothing left but the last legislation of character. What would become of us? Just as soon as our bandages were off, our unshaped lives would fall into their shapelessness!

There are thus two regions in which we may live: in the lowlands, where we ever stand in danger of the penalty of violating the law, in which we are ever conscious of the presence of the law standing over us with its drawn sword in stern warning, in which we are trying not to do wrong; and on the higher plains that breathe with blessings.

Those who live on the higher planes aim at something higher than escape from the curse of breaking the law. They strive after positive holiness. They keep far out of the reach of the curse, within the region of the Beatitudes. They stand no longer tampering with evil, looking at the forbidden fruit and parleying with the tempter, arguing as to the terms of the command laid down by God, whether it was a distinct prohibition forbidding them to eat or not. They keep well out of the reach of the forbidden tree, filling their lives so full of all that blesses that soon they have forgotten that such a tree exists.

It does indeed produce an entire change in the whole conception of the Christian life when one passes from under the law of prohibitions to live under the benign influences of the law of the Beatitudes. One ceases merely to strive against particular sins and begins truly to live and to grow in holiness. It is a veritable conversion: it makes possible what before was inconceivable; it brings the soul directly under the powers that by developing restrain it and that by giving it its true direction gently protect it from the evil influences that would destroy it.

There are those who have not yet entered into this view of life and who consequently are timid, fearful, always dreading evil that they fear will overmaster them; there is in their life little of Christian liberty and expansiveness and no joy.

A vast part of their nature remains untouched by grace. There are the germs of virtues in them that have never been developed; they hold back through fear from many a sphere of usefulness; there is a constant introspection and self-analysis; they seem never to be able to get out of themselves; they live in an atmosphere of spiritual self-consciousness. There is no such thing possible for them as self-abandonment in trustful love, but always a restless sense of insecurity; there is no confidence in God or in the power of His grace. Their thought of God is rather as judge than Savior. All through life they are haunted by a sense of failure and of unfulfilled possibilities.

Such persons are indeed strict and hard on themselves — sometimes too hard. Religion has little in it that can give them joy or peace; they are like people who are morbidly anxious about their physical health, constantly fearing illness and watching their symptoms, but never perceiving that such a condition of things makes health impossible. They are not trying to live; they are only trying not to die. Such people are unconsciously living lives of restriction and prohibition.

And then there comes a change; they pass into another atmosphere where love reigns, where positive action takes the place of mere watchfulness and self-restraint; they launch out into the deep, put forth their powers, and strive to live rather than not to die — to do good rather than not to do evil, to put forth all their strength and energy in the loving service of God and man. They live in that large sphere of positive action and aim that enables them very soon to leave far behind those evil things that they were so long striving to keep from doing. They pass upward into the life of the Beatitudes and gain a new revelation of the possibilities of religion, of its wonderful capacity of setting the soul free to live a life of ever-increasing interest and joy.

Chapter 2

Nurture Genuine Sorrow for Your Sins

The virtue which for obvious reasons we should consider first is contrition, for those who have lost their baptismal innocence can be saved only as penitents. Which of us can think that we have kept our garments in their baptismal purity? If we have not, then the foundation of our Christian character, upon which all must rest, is penitence.

So completely can this virtue stamp itself upon the whole character that we can describe many a person in one word—"penitent." Just as innocence shines out through every virtue in those few choice souls who have preserved it, and gives a special radiance and light to all they do or say, so penitence marks the whole man: it gives its own tone and color to everything; it represents to us a definite character, in spite of all else that goes to make up the character, and leaves its impress upon every virtue and grace. The other virtues get a special tone from this: the purity of St. John is different from the purity of St. Augustine. In the one it was never lost; in the other it was lost, and fought for, and regained; one had the purity of innocence, the other the purity of penitence.

Penitence, therefore, works as a great force in the soul, molding and shaping the whole character, the spring of all its movements ever acting upon the will, impelling and restraining it in all things.

And the life of penitence springs from the grace of contrition, that sorrow for sin whose source is in the love of God, whom the sinner has offended.

It begins, no doubt, in many less perfect forms. A real penitence may take its rise from the sense of one's own personal loss. "How many hired servants of my Father have bread enough and to spare, and I perish with hunger."[9] Such was the beginning of the life of penitence in the Prodigal, but it was only the beginning; it must rise higher than that. Such a sense of loss could not brace the will up; for all it has to do and to endure and to forgo, it can only lead the soul a certain way.

It can lead it back to his Father's embrace, and then it passes under the control of a stronger and more enduring power, the love of the Father, who has been offended; then it cries "Against thee only have I sinned."[10]

Thus it may be said that there are two conversions: the conversion from sin to self and the conversion from self to God. In the first stage, the thought of God is indeed present, but the sense of one's own misery and loss is the strongest. In the second, the thought of self has almost disappeared; the soul is glad to suffer, complains of nothing, rejoices if by all it has to endure it can make reparation to the love of God, against which it has sinned.

Contrition, then, in a more or less perfect form, is to be found at the very beginning of the spiritual life of all those who have ever sinned deeply. It is its first movement, that which causes

---

[9] Luke 15:17.
[10] Cf. Ps. 51:4.

it to say, "I will arise." It is the first thought that breaks in upon the soul as it awakens to the sense of its sin. "When he came to himself he said, "How many hired servants of my Father have bread enough and to spare, and I perish with hunger. I will arise and go to my Father!"

The Prodigal awakened to a sense of sin and its misery, and this produced a resolution of the will: "I will arise and go to my Father." It was the dawn of the spiritual life amidst all the squalor and degradation that sin had brought in its train.

Where the sense of sin is not, the spiritual life cannot exist; as the life of holiness grows, the spirit of contrition deepens. It seems strange, but it is undoubtedly true, that contrition deepens in proportion as the soul becomes purer, that is, in proportion as the guilt of sin is removed.

This virtue stands, then, at the entrance of the life of devotion and prayer, waiting to receive the soul and lead it onward in the pathway of holiness, and there is no grace that it does not help to form, over whose development it does not preside, and into which it does not impart something of its own stern yet gentle spirit.

If it is to exist at all, it must reign supreme and penetrate everywhere. Many a Christian virtue owes its nameless and undefined grace to the fact that its fiber has been woven by the firm yet gentle hands of contrition. It would not have grown, it never could have lived, but for the strong, tender care of that grace that can produce virtues so strangely unlike itself, so apparently opposite to itself. In a soil, barren if it had not been watered by her tears, those virtues were planted. Beneath the burning sun of temptation that would have scorched them if she had not sheltered them with her shadow, they grew and developed and blossomed, and bore fruit. Who could have ever guessed that the power that unsealed the lips of that shy, reserved person, and enabled him to speak with sympathy and love, was the deep sense of his own sin, and the longing to do something to repair its effects? Who could have guessed that the power that gave strength, determination, and perseverance to that will that never could resist temptation was the very memory of all that it had yielded to in the past, love grieving over its offenses, and restoring the power lost by sin!

Yes, we can little tell the source of the power or the immeasurable strength of the force that sets the long clogged wheels and rusted springs of the spiritual life in motion and produces such a wonderful result; and least of all is that soul in whom this grace is working such wonders, conscious of what is taking place within it. For the strange thing is that while for the penitent contrition is the mother of all virtues, she is herself the outcome of sin, and while weaving the holiest virtues, she sees how stained her hands are and seeks to wash them with her tears.

For she can never forget the past; she is the child of that past, the offspring of the mystical union between the love of God and the memory of sin; and yet the remembrance of the evil past does not hold her back or make her timid, or morbid, or over-introspective; her very strength consists in, and depends on, the perfectly healthy tone of the mind. She knows the evil of the past, but she remembers it only in the presence of her Savior, who has pardoned her. She cannot think of her sins but as forgiven, yet the very certainty of the forgiveness makes the pain of recalling them more keen, while robbing it of every vestige of morbidness or self-consciousness.

And thus there is nothing that she will not dare. She will strive after the virtues that seem to belong only to those who have been always kept pure. Despair cannot exist where she is, nor timidity. Although in another sense there is none so timid, timid she must be, remembering the past, yet not timid in the sense that she is afraid to face dangers and to aim at the very highest.

In such persons, contrition is the life and center of all the soul's strength and progress. When hope begins to get clouded, it is because contrition begins to fail. When faith grows dim and love grows cold, it is because contrition has lost her strength and is dying. Nay, so clear is her own vision of God, so certain is she of her own love, that she can encourage and sustain the soul in times of utmost darkness and deadness. At these times, contrition is up and awake, and all her strength and tenderness is expended in keeping the soul from fainting. She speaks to it again and again with accents of encouragement and inspiration. "You have deserved to lose the sense of love and clearness of faith. Why should you expect all to be clear when you remember the years in which you did not try, did not want to believe? Fight on bravely now, and the light and peace will come again."

It is at such moments that contrition shows her unfailing strength, or at times that are even worse, when old temptations come back with redoubled force, when the power of habit reasserts itself, when all the succors of grace seem to be withdrawn and the soul is left face-to-face with the multitude of her enemies, conscious only that the will has no strength to resist. Then it is that contrition comes to the rescue, and her power is felt as never before. Her power—and yet she herself seems so weak—for the inspiration of love seems to have died out of her too; yet still she is there in the thick of the fight, standing by the will, urging it on with arguments, appealing to it, strengthening it; and when every fortress of the soul seems overthrown, contrition holds the will and gains the victory.

Thus, contrition is indeed the molding and controlling force that forms, restores, and preserves the penitent. Its transforming power is so great that it can fit the greatest sinner for the company of the saints. The Magdalene was not out of place by the side of the spotless Mother. Penitence can give to the soul what it would seem could be gained only by innocence. It verily can "raise up the poor out of the dust, and lift up the beggar from the dunghill to set him among princes, and to make him inherit the throne of glory."[11]

Let us proceed to consider some of the characteristics of contrition by which we may test ourselves as to whether we are gaining any of its spirit.

Contrition Is Patient

It is ready to endure all that comes upon it, whether justly or unjustly; it knows what it deserves, and it knows that if others knew it as it truly is, it could be treated with no consideration or kindness. It recognizes that it has no rights; that the chief reason that it is permitted to live is in order that reparation may, in some degree, be done for the past. It bears about within itself an awakened conscience that speaks as the representative of the justice of the all-holy God; and the voice of conscience is ever passing sentence upon it, and the soul, in the spirit of penitence, is ever more and more ready to welcome everything as acting toward it for the satisfaction of an offended God. Nay, it longs to find new offerings to make, for it can never lose sight of God's love, and it knows that whatever it may have to suffer is not a mere penalty sent in anger, but a loving chastisement to restore and perfect it.

[11] 1 Sam. 2:8.

Nurture Genuine Sorrow for Your Sins

And it accepts above all things the consequences of past sin without a murmur, the constant presence of temptation, the sense of weakness and of loss, the deadness of heart, the poverty of prayer, the very fear of self-deception, the agony of doubt that at times darkens all the path, filling it with uncertainty, whether its penitence is real or whether, after all, it is not a specious form of self-interest.

Even this it learns to bear, and, by bearing, to overcome.

Sometimes, when tempted to doubt whether there can be pardon for one who has sinned so deeply, it triumphs by an all-enduring act of self-surrender, saying, "Well, if I am to go to hell, even that I will bear as my desert. For hell itself cannot make me cease to grieve for having offended God," and thus it conquers even the fear of hell. And it endures patiently the loss of all that it has forfeited, even its best gifts. As God has withdrawn them, it puts away the desire for them, and it knows if they are to be regained, it must be by a growing transformation of itself. It longs not so much to receive anything as to regain the love of God that it has forfeited.

And what if the power of old sin asserts itself and it yields again and falls? Even then it does not lose patience or despair but, with a deeper sense of need, strives to cling more closely to God. Despair or deep discouragement after a fall is the result of dependence on self, a subtle form of pride. True contrition knows that any moment in which the soul lets go of God, it plunges into the depths of its own weakness, and therefore if it fails, it takes the warning, saying, "Why art thou cast down O, my soul? And why art thou disquieted within me? Hope in God: for I shall yet praise him, who is the health of my countenance, and my God."[12]

---

[12] Ps. 43:5.

Contrition Is Strong

Contrition shows its strength by what it puts away rather than by what it does. It puts away those things with which it has formerly sinned. If by necessity it has them as part of its life, it puts them away from the heart.

That which has been an occasion of sin must be a memorial of sorrow. We may be violent in active antagonism to sin while we are continually recurring to objects that have been the causes of sin; but contrition puts them away, and at whatever cost. We may hate sin very much and yet feel that we must have certain things, indulgences, and friendships that have been the cause of sin in the past.

So far we are lacking in contrition. We have the element of hate, but not of love. The love of God strengthens the soul to put away from itself what has caused it to offend God. How can it love Him and enjoy what has been the means of separating it from Him?

No, it has but one great longing: to return to God: "I will arise, and go to my Father."[13] And it has one great fear: sin. "Love is stronger than death,"[14] and in the strength of love, tempered with the fear of sin, it can give up anything. No gain, no result, could make it tolerate the occasion of sin.

What strength it has to break with things that have become almost a part of our life from long habit; what strength to break with companionships that are so sweet, albeit so dangerous!

The penitent soul needs indeed to be strong, and strength is always calm. It is not merely in moments of spiritual excitement that it deals sternly with itself, relapsing into ease and self-indulgence

[13] Luke 15:18.
[14] Cf. Song of Sol. 8:6.

when the clearness of spiritual perception has passed and dullness and chill have settled down on heart and mind. No, it is as calmly firm in the darkest as in the brightest times.

When all the lower nature cries out for rest and ease, and God has withdrawn every token of His presence and love, the will remains firm in the practice of self-denial.

And again, when God grants to it moments of joy, when it has no doubt, no fear, when the assurance of its acceptance and of God's love comes upon it with an overwhelming rush of emotion, it does not permit itself to be carried away. In the midst of all that inner joy, there is the firm grasp upon itself and things around it, and it quietly perseveres in its penitential exercise. How strong it is! How faithful! How unbending toward the offender — the chief of sinners!

Contrition Is Tender

Contrition has no harshness. It springs from the love of God. It does not come before the mind as a duty; it springs out of the heart by the necessity of its own inspiration. It is the longing of a soul burdened with the sense of defilement to be conformed to the holiness of Him whom it loves. It springs from the love of God, not from the hatred of sin. We cannot rise to love by hatred, but we must pass on from the love of God to the hatred of what He hates.

The inspiration of contrition is love, not hate; there is no taint of bitterness or irritation toward self. Thus, stern and unbending in its self-discipline, it is nevertheless always tender. It bears deeply marked upon itself both the strength and the tenderness of love. It has a "heart of fire toward God, a heart of flesh toward man, a heart of steel toward self."

There is an asceticism that is harsh and stern and cruel, but it is not the asceticism of the Christian penitent. There is none so tender toward others, so sensitive for their well-being, so slow to condemn or to see others' faults. It seems to it as if all the world needs kindness and care except itself. Contrition closes the eyes toward the sins of others and opens them upon its own; it sees itself as the one culprit in the midst of a world that throbs with the love of God.

Patience, strength, tenderness! A spirit that can endow the selfish, sensual, worldly, easygoing nature with such graces must indeed be mighty. It is. It is as strong as God's justice, as gentle as His love, as patient as His mercy.

Chapter 3

⌒

Practice Mortification

Let us consider next the spirit of mortification, which is at once the necessary outcome and the guardian of contrition, for, in proportion as the spirit of mortification fails, contrition is certain to die out of the soul: and if there be no true contrition, and the soul longs to gain it, one of the surest ways is by mortification.

One whose heart is truly penitent, who lives constantly before God, confessing himself a sinner and deserving His condemnation, will instinctively put away many things from his life that are the tokens of a pleasure-loving nature. The outer life is bound to take expression from the inner, and if the penitence is deep and strong, it will not be possible but that there should be the outer tokens of it. If there are no such tokens, we must doubt the reality of the penitence.

Yet the practice of mortification is not easy. It not only makes great demands upon the will, but it needs much wisdom and prayer to practice it.

It is strange how often people are to be found who certainly practice mortification and that in no small degree, who live really ascetic lives, allowing themselves very little in the way of enjoyment or indulgence, and yet who most certainly are not mortified in the proper sense of the word, but, on the contrary, are full of self-will and a certain kind of self-indulgence.

It is necessary, therefore, that in the practice of mortification we should be quite clear what our aim ought to be and where the danger of self-deception lies, for there is no part of our nature in which self-deception acts with greater subtlety and disaster than in the higher aims of the spiritual life. It would seem almost inconceivable that a person should deny himself in many things that he liked, that he should lead a really austere life, and yet that it could be possible that all this should be a subtle form of self-indulgence, yet it undoubtedly is true. For it is unquestionably true that there may be a very wide difference between asceticism regarded as mere austerity and the Christian spirit of mortification.

There is a strange pleasure to certain temperaments in practicing self-torture: it is an end in itself, it reaches out toward nothing, grasps nothing higher; it is the morbid pleasure of inflicting pain upon oneself; it appears to be a greater pleasure to some natures to forgo what they like than to take it. This is one of those mysteries of nature that is impossible to understand, but such a spirit of mortification has nothing to do with Christianity: it is to be found all over the world, and it is often the source of the most dangerous form of pride.

But Christian mortification is wholly different in its motive and its aim. To most people, the motive from which it springs must be penitence; it is the putting away of lawful things because of past sin. The remembrance of past self-indulgence makes the soul long to forgo more and more in the spirit of reparation; it ever stands in this fair world, before God, self-condemned, and feeling that it has not the same rights that others have to the free use and enjoyment of all that is good in the world. There is nothing that it has not abused: it has allowed the creature to crowd out the thought of and the love of the Creator; therefore, in the spirit of self-condemnation, it puts away one thing after another.

In such acts of self-denial there is no harshness, no hard condemnation of the things that are put aside; on the contrary, the penitent soul realizes that the evil lies not in these things but in itself. All these things are good; they are God's creatures, but they have been abused, and they are put aside with an ever-deepening feeling of its own unworthiness. It feels keenly how sin has marred the order of God's creation, has put man in a false relation to all these things. It has given them a hold upon him; he has sunk under their influence; they have enslaved him. He has allowed them, instead of raising him to God, to drag him down and to blind him so that he cannot see God.

Consequently, there is no condemnation of those things that he willingly forgoes; indeed, the mind becomes purified by penitence, so as to see deeper into their meaning and their beauty, and to appreciate their real value more. In stripping itself of all that is fairest in the world, the penitent soul looks upon the world not with the jaundiced eye of Puritanism but with a tender love, weeping over his own sin and weakness, which make him incapable of using what, had he been truer, he might have used and, in using, risen through them to God.

Nor does he condemn others who do not put away things that he does; no, he feels that his own position is an exceptional one: he is a penitent, one who has abused God's good gifts and therefore does not deserve nor dare to have them. But with others it is different; others, he feels, are not like him, and while stripping himself more and more of all but the barest necessities, he will with the utmost tenderness try to protect others from the deprivations he practices himself.

And thus, penitence as the motive for mortification protects him who practices it from hardness and pride on the one hand, and, on the other, from a false condemnation of those things that he surrenders, as if they were evil in themselves. As he loosens himself from the dominion of the creatures that had enslaved and blinded him, he understands and appreciates as he never did before their value and their beauty, and he perceives how it is possible for man to rise through them to God. It is impossible, therefore, to condemn them as evil; he has traced evil to its true source and has found that it lies in his own heart and will.

Thus, in the most mortified and ascetic life, amidst the barest surroundings, stripped of all save the merest necessities, living in the utmost poverty (like Him of whom it was said: "The foxes have holes, and the birds of the air have nests, but the Son of man hath not where to lay his head"[15]), amidst circumstances as hard and stern as these, the Christian displays the most perfect tenderness and gentleness of heart, the clearest sense of the real value of all things, the most intense appreciation of the beauty of nature and the profoundest humility. The school of self-discipline and mortification in which he has placed himself has done its work and has proved that it is based on a true principle by the wonderful blending of the most opposite virtues, gentleness and strength, self-condemnation and appreciation of others — the putting away as evil for him what is valued and esteemed more and more as good in itself.

If there were any trace of bitterness, any faintest taint of Manichean condemnation of God's creatures, any hardness toward those who were not led to a similar life of mortification, we

---

[15] Matt. 8:20.

might condemn it, as based upon a wrong principle, but when we see the result, we cannot but feel that a principle producing such results must be founded on truth.

But the spirit of mortification does not spring from penitence alone; it grows out of the condition of our life here on earth. It is necessary for all who would be true to God and to themselves. As man was originally created, God was supreme Master of his heart and will. He saw — he knew — his end: to love God above all things and to serve Him. And he found himself in a world beautiful and attractive, in which every created thing spoke to him of God and pointed him upward. His nature had many needs, and he found around him all that would supply these needs, provided by the loving hand of God; and in satisfying the wants of nature, he was drawn more closely to God. His eye was, as it were, illuminated, so that it could pierce through all and see God in all. He took what his nature needed with unerring instinct and without fear or danger of indulgence; all was in order within him and without, and God was over all and in all.

But with the Fall all this was changed. Man chose the creature before the Creator, and the creatures enslaved and blinded him. He no longer found that created things lifted him up to God, but that they became an end in themselves. By the order of his creation he needed the creatures; he could not live without them, for they were meant to lead him constantly to God. But now they came between him and God and held him down. As he used them, he found himself more and more blinded and enslaved by them. His whole relationship to them was overthrown, the balance was lost; he could no longer see clearly the meaning and purpose of things nor rise through them to God; his will got entangled and his senses ensnared.

Spiritual Principles for Souls Seeking God

The instinct that guided him was gone. Earlier he moved about amidst things that lifted his whole being Godward, into the mystery of whose existence he saw as into a crystal stream. Now he moves amongst them as one fascinated and bewildered. He finds himself guided in the choice or rejection of things by their appearances and their power of giving pleasure, not by the only true principle, their effects in leading him to or holding him back from God. And thus he judges things by their immediate effects upon himself, and finding in them the power of satisfying many wants of his nature, he takes all that his unbalanced nature desires and does not perceive that created things are gaining a faster and tighter grip upon him, till they fill the whole horizon of his soul and shut out God. And as time goes on, every step onward creates new wants that Nature supplies from her exhaustless treasury, and the satisfaction of all these wants binds man more fast to earth and to its creatures.

How quickly they ensnare, how easily they blind, how rapidly our needs increase we all know but too well. The man of many needs crowds round his life such vast supplies of earthly and material things that the heart becomes deadened and ceases even to desire spiritual things. How can it rise, bound down on every side?

Yet all these things are in themselves good; they are indeed meant to be channels of approach to God—revelations of God—but the channels have become clogged, the creatures have become opaque, and at last they form a barrier between the soul and God.

Therefore, we have to keep ourselves loose from creatures. We have to learn to use them as they were meant to be used, as means to an end, and the end is God. We have to use each thing as it comes, to use it or abstain from its use insofar as it leads us to God. If anything helps us Godward, it should be used so far as, neither more nor less than, it leads to God. They are means to an end, and such is the nature of those things that are means or instruments that we should consider, in regard to them, if they are (and to what extent they are) useful as instruments for the end for which we propose to use them.

We have a difficult task before us. We are obliged to use many things that have in them a most remarkable and strange power of working their way into our lives and enslaving us, and we have to learn so to use them as to keep free from their dominion and to rise through them to God.

To do this, we need to hold ourselves well in hand, conquering those things that try to conquer us — not allowing ourselves to go to the verge of self-indulgence, but keeping ourselves more and more free from the dominion of those things that were created to be our servants, not our masters. We must learn to gauge our progress, not by the multiplying of our needs but by minimizing them. He who could feed the multitude in the wilderness and calm the storm on the lake said of Himself, "The foxes have holes, and the birds of the air have nests; but the Son of man hath not where to lay his head."[16] He who could rule the creatures would not permit them to rule Him. He deliberately set them aside and lived in poverty.

What a perversion of ideas it is that we should look upon as great those who accumulate around themselves riches and all kinds of luxuries, and consequently multiply their needs. They are not, after all, the masters but the servants of the creatures that rule them. Our Lord's estimate of greatness and true

---

[16] Matt. 8:20.

happiness was different: "Blessed are the poor in spirit: for theirs is the kingdom of heaven."[17]

And all this, standing in the right attitude toward creatures, needs the constant practice of mortification, the holding of heart and will free for God. As we find a thing getting too strong a hold upon us, it is not easy to draw back and keep it in check. Food, sleep, pleasure, and a thousand other things: as we touch them, they enchant us and call upon us to give in to their enjoyment as much as we desire. The effort to keep all these things in their place involves a mortified life. To stop short of indulgence, to drive away something that we are afraid is beginning to enslave us until we have taught it its proper place and admit it again later into our life as a useful servant; to stand amidst the vast multitude of God's creatures with which the earth teems—persons, places, things, sorrows, joys, pleasure, and pains—a free man, enslaved by none but using all fearlessly, neither held back by fear nor attracted by mere pleasure, but using and accepting or rejecting each as it comes, insofar as it leads the soul Godward—this is indeed liberty; but such liberty can be purchased only by mortification.

And such liberty cannot be gained by the mere action of a determined will. No, the will needs a lever to raise nature out of the bondage to creatures. And where shall such a lever be found? The power strongest to move the will is love. And there is but one love that can counteract the attraction of creatures: the love of Him who being God took unto Himself a created nature, the sum and consummation of all creatures.

We turn to Him; we cling to His human nature. He is the way—out of the labyrinth in which we are entangled—to the

[17] Matt. 5:3.

Father. As our love for the man Christ Jesus grows more and more within us, we feel an attraction that lifts us from the earth and gives the soul once more its balance. We submit ourselves to the slavery of His love, whom to serve is to reign. "If the Son therefore shall make you free, ye shall be free indeed."[18]

---

[18] John 8:36.

Chapter 4

⌒

Discover Your Particular Vocation

There is nothing sadder to see than an aimless life. Such a life does not necessarily mean that the person who lives it never has an aim, but that the aim is constantly being changed. Many a day may be lived very intensely: sometimes an object of interest may fill and absorb every thought for several days. Indeed, it is surprising the amount of force and enthusiasm that is expended upon some passing interest altogether out of proportion to its value. Yet a life with all these changing interests and excitements may, after all, be an utterly aimless life. Its characteristic is that it is taken up with passing things, not with anything that is permanent.

The chief bond that binds such a life together is its most marked characteristic—changeableness, instability, uncertainty.

For it is the end—the aim—that interprets the life. We judge people not so much by their attainments as by the tendency, the bent of their life. One may use great and excellent gifts for some unworthy purpose, and even though the purpose may never be attained, we know that it has demoralized the character. We judge one another not so much by what we are as by what we are becoming, trying to be. A person who aims at some noble end in life is noble; the difference between the commonplace life and that which is above the commonplace lies mainly in the region of motive. Before you can understand why one man, with all his failures and blunders, is so different from another, who is in many things more successful, you must understand what it is that inspires his life. The person whose life from first to last is inspired by the noblest aim, however constantly it may fail, however devoid it may be of the brilliancy of natural gifts, lives the noblest of lives.

What, then, ought to be the aim that inspires the whole character of one who would live the best and noblest life on earth? Many things at once occur to us that would appeal to ambition and call for applause, some necessitating one great gift, some another, but the greatest and most perfect life does not necessarily require great gifts — it lies open to all.

It has, not rarely, been lived by those who have been below the average so far as natural endowments are concerned. It is, indeed, a wonderful homage to the power of a great motive to stamp itself upon and develop character that there are not a few whose names are known in history only on this account, who otherwise would have been lost in the crowd of the commonplace; but they were lifted up and made great by the motive that formed and governed their lives.

And what motive, then, lies open to all, can be followed equally by all, and makes all great who follow it?

It seems a very simple one, yet it involves much: it is to fulfill as perfectly as possible the purpose for which one was created by God and placed here upon earth. "As God hath distributed to every man, as the Lord hath called every one, so let him walk."[19]

---

[19] 1 Cor. 7:17.

Discover Your Particular Vocation

No one can do better with his life than that; no one can put it to a better use. Any life must be perfect in proportion as it does what it was made to do. There are many lives that are brilliant failures; they strive after many things that they were never intended to do and fail in that one thing. It seems strange that a reasonable being should never ask himself why he was put upon earth, or that it should not occur to him that the reason must be found in the will of his Creator.

I employ a man to do a certain piece of work for me at a certain price. He comes to me at the end of the day and says, "I have been very busy all day; I have spent all my time in doing some work of my own that I was anxious to finish." I answer, "But you have not done the work that I employed you to do; you have been full of your own plans, not mine; therefore, I shall not pay you."

At the end of the day of our earthly life, we have to answer to our Maker whether we have been employed about our own work or about His, whether we have even made an effort to find out what He would have us do.

A life that is inspired by such a motive is sure to be a success, for of this we may be absolutely certain: that each of us can fulfill in our life that for which we were created. We cannot be sure that we have the gifts needed for any other purpose—there is at least a risk about it—but in this there is no risk. For God, in creating us, equipped us for the work for which He created us. We have every gift of nature and of grace, of mind and body that is needed for this work.

These gifts can no doubt be used for other ends, and the more brilliant they are, the more diverse the uses to which they can be put. Many, not caring to find out what they were given for, may altogether abuse them or use them for purposes that can never develop them to their full capacity, and consequently the character of the person who possesses them will suffer, and the life will fall short of real success.

Often the source of discontent, and restlessness, and lack of peace in a life that, from its power and influence and many gifts, is the envy of others is the half consciousness that the aim is not right, that the powers are not being used for the purpose for which they were given.

It will be an inspiring thought, then, to keep before us: I have all the powers necessary for a true success in life; no one is so fitted as I am to do the special work I have to do, to fill the special place that I have to fill. God wished a certain work to be done; He is almighty and all wise; He saw exactly the person best fitted to do it. He might have created one endowed with every conceivable gift, but He created me; He knew what He was about — it was no accident. I did not come here by chance, but as the result of an intelligent will. We may try after something that is more to our taste or showier or that calls for less exertion and discipline, and so may fail. Or we may live in total forgetfulness that we were put here on earth for any purpose at all, or we may waste our life and gifts in fretful discontent with the lot that we are powerless to escape. But if we take as the key to life the will of God and strive to realize His purpose in our creation and then to fulfill it, we *must* succeed; and that success will crown the character with a beauty, an attractiveness, a harmony, and an inward peace that will leave the soul without a doubt that the end is right.

Then, too, God has withheld from us what would not be serviceable to this end; it is in His goodness that He has not overweighed the soul with what would be useless or with what might dissipate its strength or obstruct its path.

Discover Your Particular Vocation

There are many gifts that we may envy in others, yet if we had them, they would be only a hindrance; if they were necessary for us, God would have given them to us. We do not stud the handle of a hammer with precious stones; if we did, we would be afraid to use it for its ordinary work; and God has not so encrusted our nature with gifts and talents as to blind us to its real purpose.

By this means life is made simpler; many doors are closed at the outset: we feel, or we ought to feel, shut out of various positions and spheres of work or influence that pride or ambition might call us into. Indeed, we know well how difficult it is often to accept our limitations; and how many people spend their lives trying to push their way through doors that are very clearly closed against them, but they will not believe it.

Thus, each of us has all that is necessary for fulfilling God's purpose in life, and what we have not we need not regret or envy in others. God did not withhold anything in a grudging spirit, but only because it would be in our way.

And the work of life that God calls us to do has one great end: the development and perfecting of our character. It has, no doubt, its own intrinsic value; it would be a most uninspiring view of the work of life to suppose that in itself it was worthless, like some piece of work given a child, only to teach her how to use her needle. We cannot estimate the value of what is done upon earth; we cannot see its issues; but that it has an intrinsic value we cannot doubt.

Yet the great end for which *we* have been chosen to do it is for our own development and perfection. We may no doubt do the very work God has put us on earth to do in a way that injures ourselves; but if this be so, we may also feel assured that the work of God must suffer also; if the machine gets out of order, it cannot do its work perfectly.

Spiritual Principles for Souls Seeking God

It is by the work of life and in the place chosen by God, that the character is to be formed and perfected, and it is by the character deepening in perfection that the work is to be most perfectly done. There is the work, and there is the man—they were made for one another—no one can do the work so well as he, and no other work can do so much for that man.

Such a thought will give interest and value to all we have to do and will raise the smallest and most insignificant duties out of the commonplace. Those uninteresting surroundings and dull people and that round of duties are the tools with which God carves and chisels out of our nature the likeness of Christ. To neglect anything, to do anything in a careless and perfunctory way, will not only spoil the work but will injure the worker.

This, then, must be a fundamental and ruling principle in life: the principle of vocation—of a purpose that we are called to fulfill. Everything will go wrong if the aim is not right. If the aim is true, it will give force and directness to the whole character, and every power of nature and grace will be developed in its perfect proportion.

The idea of vocation must not be limited to one or two of the more clearly marked calls of God, such as the call to the priesthood or the religious life; we read in the Gospels of one who thought he had a call to such a special following of our Lord as the Apostles had, and our Lord forbade him and said to him, "Go home to thy friends, and tell them of the great things the Lord hath done for thee."[20] He would have mistaken his vocation if he had given up everything to follow Christ; his vocation, therefore, was as distinctly to the home life as was St. Peter's to the apostolic life.

[20] Cf. Mark 5:19.

Discover Your Particular Vocation

It is important that we should remember this: vocation is the call of God to whatever form of life He may please to call one. The *realizing* of one's position in life *as a vocation* is like a conversion; it is the opening of the eyes to see the purpose and will of God behind and through the ordinary events of life. The parable of the laborers in the vineyard shows us the monotonous and commonplace life of a day laborer transformed by the hearing of the call, "Go, work in my vineyard."[21]

In the manifold works and obligations of life, in all that keeps the world going, the fundamental difference lies in this: that multitudes who fulfill those duties do so because they are obliged; some few do them in obedience to the will of God, and this makes all the difference in the character of those who work. Therefore, while some vocations are no doubt more clearly marked than others, everyone, no matter how humble his position, has his place and work assigned by God, and consequently has in the true sense of the word a vocation, the realizing and fulfilling of which is the condition of perfection.

We must consider further that all God's action toward us will be directed to perfect us through our vocation: "This is the will of God, even your sanctification."[22] It is true that He does care for our happiness and temporal welfare. Everything that affects us is of interest to Him, but all is subservient to our true happiness and the real success of life. If health is necessary that we should reach this end, we may be assured that we shall have health; if health would hinder us, it shall be taken from us. If success is good for us, He will allow us to succeed, but if it would stand in

---

[21] Cf. Matt. 20:4.
[22] 1 Thess. 4:3.

our way, if we would rest in it or it would elate us and make us worldly, we shall not have success.

And so with everything: all is in His hands, and all is ordered with a view to this one end — the fulfilment of the purpose for which He placed us here.

And God cannot be won over to forgo this. No prayers will move Him. He would be unfaithful to us and to His promises if He failed to fulfill His part. The opportunities, the temptations, the troubles, the blessings will come, the ordering of the outward circumstances of our life; all this we may be sure of, whether we respond properly or not. This mighty will goes on ordering all, just as it would if we were faithful.

There is something at once alarming and bracing in this thought: it is alarming, indeed, if we do not care to respond, to think that the strong currents of God's will, working toward an end from which we have turned away, still keep beating around us, beating upon us, filling the spaces of our life with movements that all tend in the opposite direction to our own, and that must eventually crush us if we do not turn and yield.

And yet bracing, too: is it not a bracing and inspiring thought to think that there is the will of Him who orders all things toward one end — the end toward which we have turned our life — and that it is always on the side of our best selves, always waging unceasing war against any one-sided or partial view of life; that if we get lax or weak, He will not be so unkind as to yield to us; that if we swerve for an instant to one side or the other, it, as it were, strikes us and forces us back again. What a strength to think that we have no plan, no purpose in life but His whose will orders all things.

We have thus but to look out upon the circumstances of our life at any moment to see the operation of this will on our behalf.

"All things work together for good"[23] if only our will is directed toward the same end as His. A few suggestions may be helpful with a view to training the will to correspond with God's purpose.

- *Try to see the will of God in little things.* "The very hairs of your head are numbered."[24] "Not a sparrow shall fall to the ground"[25] without His will. Nothing happens in our daily life without His permitting it, even what happens through the sin of others. God does not will sin, but He does permit that, sin being committed, we should be tried by it. It needs the constant exercise of faith and watchfulness to see the will of God constantly operating toward us.

- *Keep the will free when anything naturally pleasing offers itself,* some opportunity of enjoyment, some plan that you would naturally like. Wait before you decide and look to God; consult His will before you choose. That pause and prayer may make all the difference in the result of your choice.

- *So, too, in times of uncertainty, make constant acts of self-oblation.* Keep your will free until you know the will of God. Many a time such periods of uncertainty are permitted as times of preparation. During that time of waiting, the will learns to accept what it perhaps could not have accepted at once.

- *Do not throw too much intensity into the legitimate choices of the will in ordinary things that give enjoyment.* Hold much of

---

[23] Rom. 8:28.
[24] Luke 12:7.
[25] Cf. Matt. 10:29.

the power of the will in reserve; don't spend and exhaust its powers in things that are not worth it. With certain temperaments the tendency is to choose passionately and with all the intensity of one's nature the passing pleasures or superficial things of life as well as the deeper and more important. Consequently, there is a lack of proper detachment and readiness to forgo what one may have to give up. Keep yourself in hand and reserve the whole power of the will's choice for those things that are worth it.

• *Remember, there is a vast difference between willing and wishing*; you can't help what you wish at any given moment, but your will is in your own power. Your wishes are the inclinations of your nature, as you find them now, from whatever cause — temperament, taste, or perhaps past sin. It can't be helped now, but often the greatest triumphs of grace consist in the will's choosing in direct opposition to what nature wishes. You can't help wishing not to say your prayers, or not to fast, or not to get up in the morning, but you can *will* and determine to act in opposition to these wishes and so to grow in strength and grace. Therefore, don't be anxious because many times you don't *wish* to do God's will — *will* to do it, *do* it, and the triumph and the reward will be all the greater.

And so, in spite of, and through, all the obstacles, both within and without, that beset the pathway of the soul, it presses on to fulfill the purpose of God.

Chapter 5

⌒

Reap the Spiritual Bounty of Sacrifice

There are many things that belong to man's life on earth in his fallen state that will cease with his earthly condition. Much of his life and thought is necessarily taken up with such things. It is a strange contrast that is presented by the seriousness of life as we are taught it in Holy Scripture and the multitude of trifles and superficial things that fill up the days of so many of us, yet no doubt all these things have their value in the discipline of character.

And there are many virtues that can be developed only under the present conditions of life, such as faith, contrition, and patience, although these virtues, rooted deeply in our nature, will bear their perfect fruits in eternity. What the effect of an ever-deepening penitence on earth will be when the soul has been cleansed from every consequence of sin and sees God face-to-face through eternity, we cannot tell. Or what the result will be of the discipline of a life of faith when faith is lost in vision, we cannot tell. Or what place an enduring patience that has been fought for so bravely here can have in the soul that can never again be thwarted or tried, we do not know. We can readily see, however, that one trained in such a school, when he passes upward out of the present condition of things, bears within him a certain tone of character that can develop, under other circumstances, into other types of perfection of which these may be but the seeds and roots, just as there seems but little connection between the lessons and discipline of the schoolroom and the developed powers of some great statesman or artist.

It may perhaps be that all those virtues that especially belong to our condition here on earth will develop into the one perfect and many-sided grace of love — a love that has been tested in every conceivable way and comes forth from the fires purified and unchangeable.

But there are some ruling principles of the Christian life whose continuity we can see more clearly; there are virtues and practices begun here that are to be continued through eternity. Worship, praise, adoration, the love of and submission to the will of God — these and many other such habits are to be exercised forever. Here, indeed, they are to be learned under circumstances that form our probation; there they are to be our joy.

But there is an orderly growth and development in these graces; the soul that struggles with itself against all that would lead it away, to cling to and obey the will of God, will find its eternal joy in living beneath the perfect rule of that will; all that is counter to it will have passed away, and it will know that to serve Him is to reign. So again, the efforts after worship and praise amidst all the distractions and temptations of life, prompted and supported by faith, will be crowned by the glorious worship of heaven in the full vision of God.

Habits are being formed here under the pressure of temptation and difficulty that unfold in perfect form and beauty when the soul that has developed these habits passes into its true home. Those very temptations that made it so difficult to persevere were really the means of developing these powers. The spirit of prayer and worship grew on; hampered and oppressed by the distractions of life, it fought its way in spite of them and thus gained strength; then, when all these were removed, it opened out unhindered in its perfect growth.

Now, there is one fundamental principle of the spiritual life that has to be learned and practiced here, mostly with suffering, often with the very keenest suffering, sometimes even involving the sacrifice of life itself; and yet suffering, although so closely associated with it that it almost seems a necessary part of it, is indeed only accidental, and one day will altogether cease, while the grace that has been fought for and developed in so much agony will live on forever, and be the delight of the soul through eternity. I mean the principle of sacrifice and self-oblation.

In the worship described in the vision in the book of Revelation, "the four and twenty elders fall down before him that sat upon the throne and worship him that liveth for ever and ever, and cast their crowns before the throne."[26] They lay their crowns, the symbol of their attainments, at the feet of Him who sits upon the throne; and while these glorified saints are thus offering themselves in delighted homage in heaven amidst surroundings that tell of perfect joy and peace, some poor struggling Christian upon earth has broken away with tears and an aching heart from what he loves most, that he may do more thoroughly what he believes to be the will of God. The principle that moves both is the same — sacrifice and self-oblation — only here on earth the will is being purified and cleansed, loosening itself with pain from the creatures to which it clings inordinately, so that in faith and often with little sensible love, it may give itself to God.

[26] Rev. 4:10.

There, in that picture in heaven, we see the result; there is no more need of struggle or effort: the will is free, bound forever to the will of God, and it is the joy of the soul for eternity to cast itself and all it possesses at the feet of its Creator.

Suffering, in our present state, is indeed an integral part of the life of sacrifice, so much so that we scarcely think of sacrifice as apart from suffering; but it is good for us, when we are called upon to make the most painful sacrifice, to remember that there is no necessary connection between the two ideas.

Originally there certainly was none. When Adam stood in Eden, clad in the garment of original righteousness, and cast himself in worship before God, it was his greatest joy to offer himself; there was no obstacle between him and God to hold him back, no barrier obstructing the will through which it had to force its way.

And certainly the hosts of angels knew no life apart from God and have no will save His; yet their life of heavenly joy and peace, into which no pain or discord has ever entered, is a life of sacrifice.

So far as we know, there is but one spot in creation where there is any association between suffering and sacrifice, or where there is associated with obeying the will of God any idea of difficulty or pain, and that is here on earth. For here sin has entered and set up barriers between man and God; but we look backward and forward, and we see that originally it was not so, and hereafter it shall not be so.

Such a condition belongs only to our present state; here we must fight our way in spite of all the obstacles that seek to hold us back from doing God's will, knowing that whatever it costs us, it is our only true life and that the struggle and the pain are the conditions of our regaining our true relationship to Him and forever rejoicing in His will.

Reap the Spiritual Bounty of Sacrifice

We may look up, then, when conscience calls us to make some great and painful sacrifice and say, "The pain only belongs to my present state; countless multitudes of my fellow creatures find such acts of sacrifice their greatest joy, the pain will soon cease, for the will will soon know that its completest life is in following the will of God; meanwhile, every struggle and painful choice for God helps to restore the balance that sin has destroyed, turning the will away from the Creator to the creature."

It is, then, in following the will of God, in spite of all the difficulties that may arise both from within and from without, in the constant offering of ourselves to God as the creatures of His hand to do and to be what He would have us, in the surrender of one thing after another that comes between us and Him and holds us back—it is in such acts that we unite ourselves with those glorious beings who cast their crowns before the throne and with those unfallen creatures who have never known what it is to have a wish or thought apart from the will of God.

Amongst those glorified saints there are, indeed, many whose wills were for a long time in revolt against God's will and who brought themselves at last into subjection, many to whom the will of God here on earth meant the sacrifice of everything the heart most loved, many to whom it meant the sacrifice of life itself.

But all that is past and over, and its fruits alone remain—the eternal life of oblation and union with God, where one will rules those countless multitudes and binds them together and to God, where each one of those countless millions lives his own complete and perfect life yet never jars on any other, where each is perfect in itself and all together compose one perfect whole—the Body of Christ.

This is the outcome of that life of sacrifice and discipline on earth; it is for this that the will has to be so constantly broken, and that God demands of us what costs so much, every act of painful sacrifice helping to cleanse the will of its obstinacy, selfishness, adherence to creatures, until, brought completely under the control of God, the soul is ready to take its place in the glorified Body.

Or, to put it in another way, man was created under the law of sacrifice. It is the fundamental law of the creature's life to surrender himself wholly to his Creator's will. In fulfilling this law, he found his own perfection and his own completest happiness. Then came the Fall, when man fell from his life of union with God, and chose the creature rather than the Creator, and thus gave creatures a power over him that they did not have originally and raised up barriers between him and God. But still the law of his life remained; his truest happiness and his only perfection consisted in living the life of self-oblation.

But now all kinds of difficulties beset his path if he would live this life; much of his time had to be taken up, if he would live, in things that concerned only the present and seemed to have no relation to God or the future; the penalty inflicted upon him at his expulsion from Eden—"in the sweat of thy face shalt thou eat bread"[27]—bound together the preservation of his life with labor.

If he would not work, he could not eat; and what connection could there be between such labor and the worship of God? Its tendency was, as we know too well, to drag him down and make him less spiritual. The life of toil does drag down and weary the mind, and it is hard for the laborer to realize as he goes forth day after day to his work and to his labor until the evening, that this nature, which seems to fit itself so aptly to the life of the beast of

---

[27] Gen. 3:19.

burden, was made for worship and for God. Yet, however worn out and wearied with toil, however clouded the mind may be with care and too tired to think, the law of man's life still remains unchanged; his only true happiness and perfection is to be found in the life of sacrifice.

But not only did this law of labor make it difficult for him to live the life of worship and oblation; there were other difficulties that beset his path at every step. There is opposition coming from others, sometimes inspired by hate, sometimes by the love of those who would hold him back by their tenderness from doing what seemed so hard. There are often conflicting claims of duty when the rights of others seemed to stand in the way of fulfilling what appeared to be the will of God. And there are those countless trials that clip the wings that would soar upward, dragging the soul down to earth, the irritations and sorenesses that spring from the thoughtlessness of others, the lack of sympathy that makes life so chill, the miserable mistakes by which the most ill-assorted lives are bound together, bringing in their train a multitude of temptations that rob the soul of any power to rise to God, the irresponsiveness of those we would help, and the countless worries and vexations that cloud the atmosphere and drive the soul steadily downward to earth. Certainly many who recognize the law of self-oblation have found it so difficult to fulfill that they have given it up as hopeless.

And then our Lord came, the second Adam, into a world that was disordered by the sin of the first Adam, to show us how to live on earth amidst all these altered conditions true to the primary law of the creature's life. He did not exempt Himself from any of the conditions under which man has to live; He came to show us how it was possible to live amidst all these difficulties the perfect life of sacrifice.

He came down from the midst of the perfect worship of heaven, assumed our nature, and lived in it from His birth to His death, in absolute obedience to the great vow of the incarnation, "Lo, I come to do thy will, O God."[28] Such was the motto of His life, and He carried it out perfectly and without swerving, even though every obstacle that man or devil could devise was thrown in His way.

But those very efforts to hinder Him were made the means by which the will of God was worked out. There was, indeed, but one place where any real obstacle could be raised, and that was in the will of Him who came to offer Himself; unless that failed, nothing else could really hinder Him.

We watch Him, then, entering into the life we know so well and passing through those troubles and temptations that have held so many down; and we see Him press on, although obstacle after obstacle was thrown across His path, but still He never swerves. Sometimes He has to wait, sometimes to hold back, sometimes to retire, but never for a moment does He swerve, and rarely if ever does God intervene in the natural order of events to help Him. No, He must live as we live, under the same conditions, not a life surrounded or protected by miracles.

Men are free: they may listen to or scorn Him; they may try to make Him a king or kill Him; God leaves the world and leaves His Son, as He leaves us, to fight His way through it, and to answer by His life, not merely by His words, how in such a world man can live true to the law of the creature's life.

At times the difficulties were so great that it seemed as if it would prove impossible to carry out His purpose. Misunderstanding, misrepresentation, unfaithful friends, treachery, deliberate

---

[28] Heb. 10:7.

injustice, envy, organized opposition, the slowness of perception of His own most faithful followers, the narrow prejudice of His hearers. On all sides difficulties sprang up, apparently making it impossible for Him to carry out the work He came on earth to do, until finally He was arrested and brought to trial and condemned to death. But meanwhile, within His most holy soul, His human will was ever pressing through all these difficulties upward toward God. His will pierced through these things that were meant to hinder Him, and they all formed so many elements in His life of sacrifice.

Can anything hinder Him?

No, for the very obstacles are transformed. They were meant by Satan to block the pathway of the will Godward, but that strong, loving will forced its way through them and rose, and the effort and struggle enhanced the value of the offering.

See Him at last as He hangs upon the Cross — the one great sacrifice of the world, the sacrifice that we constantly plead upon our altars, the central act of our worship. This it was that was prefigured in the gorgeous ritual of the Temple; it is upon this that we alone rest our hopes, through it alone that we can ever approach God or offer an acceptable prayer.

Yet did it look like a great act of worship?

No, it looked to all appearances to be but a terrible scene of cruelty and crime. And so it was; everything that the eye could see or the ear could hear was low, degraded.

Was it amidst such scenes, such sounds, that God could be worshipped? It seems a degradation that any noble life should be exposed to such scenes of shame. Yet even there, amidst that vile base mob, the offscourings of the slums of Jerusalem, amidst jeers and blasphemies, the most sublime act of worship and sacrifice ascended before God that had ever been offered on this earth.

Nay, more, those very things that crowd around the cross of shame, the words, the deeds, the acts of cruelty, they form, so to speak, the instruments for the offering of this divine liturgy. Rising through all, transforming, hallowing all, was the pure will of Him who hung upon the Cross, accepting, offering all to God, and using the sins of men and the pain and humiliation that their sins brought upon Him as elements by which the value of His offering was enhanced.

Yes, by stooping so low, by permitting Himself to be the victim of all that hatred and envy, He shows us that there are no circumstances so low, no trials so humiliating, that they cannot be transformed by the will that rises through them and offers them to God.

This, then, is the lesson of our Lord's life and Passion. All difficulties, all sufferings, all obstacles that cross our path to hinder us from offering ourselves to God—all these are to be looked upon as the instruments of our sacrifice: we are to use them, to rise through them. The will forcing its way through such opposition makes the sacrifice costlier.

In the sacrifice of our Lord there were things both great and small—the teasing thorns and the cruel nails, the jarring voices of the ignorant mob, and the cold-blooded villainy of Caiaphas.

So it is with us, things great and small take their part in consummating our sacrifice: the irritations arising from those we live with who do not understand us or who are not congenial, the cutting word that wounds our pride, the weariness and monotony of life's routine, the drag of our earthly nature that will not rise, the uninteresting, unexciting, commonplace duties, ill health—all these things and a thousand more that torment us day by day and seem sometimes to take all power of resistance from us; and the greater trials—strong temptations, bitter disappointments, failures, sorrow, bodily pain, loss of friends—all these tend to keep the will down or to rouse it to revolt. But as we struggle through them, making acts of oblation and acceptance, clinging, while the lower nature cries out in pain, still clinging to God and offering them up, then we are following the lesson of our Lord's life, using life's difficulties as the instruments of our sacrifice.

Every time we offer up the Holy Sacrifice, we should offer it with deeper meaning; we should bring its lessons into our daily life and learn to live the life of sacrifice. It was the genius of sanctity that transformed that which had been the symbol of shame into the symbol of all that is noblest, holiest, and highest, and we in our measure and degree as we draw closer to Him can transform the lowest, poorest, most humbling of our troubles by the way we bear it, seeing in every trial a part of our cross, an instrument of our passion, looking forward to that eternal life beyond, where countless myriads live the life of perfect oblation and cast their crowns before the throne with the joy and peace that has been gained through the cross and sufferings of earth.

Chapter 6

⌒

Deepen Your Friendship with God

The perfect life consists in the perfect correspondence to the will of God. He who came to teach us how to live said, "I came down from heaven, not to do my own will, but the will of Him that sent me";[29] "My meat is to do the will of him that sent me, and to finish his work";[30] and St. Paul says of Him, "Even Christ pleased not himself."[31]

In the hour of His agony, His prayer was, "If it be possible, let this cup pass from me; nevertheless, not as I will, but as thou wilt."[32] He would not anticipate by a moment the appointed work of His life. "My hour is not yet come,"[33] He said again and again; but when the hour had come for work or suffering, He never failed.[34] From first to last, His life was the perfect correspondence with His Father's will. His first word was: "Did you

---

[29] Cf. John 6:38.
[30] John 4:34.
[31] Rom. 15:3.
[32] Matt. 26:39.
[33] Cf. John 2:4.
[34] John 2:4; 8:20; 13:1.

not know, that I must be about my Father's business?"[35] Almost His last was: "It is finished."[36]

Therefore, the more truly we desire to follow our Lord's example and to attain perfection, the more deeply must this principle underlie all our plans and actions. As we lose sight of this, we are almost certain to get astray and set up false standards and unworthy aims.

But such a life involves great self-discipline and constant sacrifice; many an ambition has to be crushed, many an opening for plans that are much to our taste has to be abandoned. Any who would live such a life must have their nature well in hand and be living in close communion with God. It is an easy thing to say, "The perfect life is the perfect correspondence with the will of God," but it is not easy to carry out in practice, for it is certain to lead us along a rough and difficult path where oftentimes our heart and strength will fail us. If it was so with the Master, we cannot be surprised that it should be the same with the servant.

There are two things especially that any who would live this life will need. First, the ever-increasing knowledge of God's will; and, secondly, the grace to correspond with it when it is known; first, light and secondly, grace — light for the mind, grace for the will. We may know God's will for us well enough at any given moment and not have the strength to obey it, or we may at times earnestly desire to follow God's will and yet not know it. We need both light and grace.

Now, so that we may attain these gifts, it is necessary to be living near God. It is impossible for us to turn suddenly from a

[35] Luke 2:49, Douay-Rheims.
[36] John 19:30.

distracted or careless life and to find ourselves at once illuminated and strengthened. The knowledge of God's will is often most difficult to attain, even for those living very near Him; often those who love Him most and are most single-minded are left in doubt as to His purpose for them, and only by constant prayer and self-discipline do they gradually gain the knowledge.

Therefore, if we would not make grievous mistakes and perhaps make shipwreck of our lives, we must endeavor to keep near to God, to learn to know Him better, to understand the tokens of His will and the method of His dealings with us; in a word, to get on terms of loving and reverent friendship with Him.

But this can be done only by prayer. A prayerful life is almost certainly a life of conformity to the will of God; a prayerless life is quite certainly a life of self-will, in which imperfections and sins and the spirit of worldliness cloud the spiritual perception so that it is not even conscious of how far it is separated from God.

And yet, while prayer is the condition of knowing God, there is no practice of the spiritual life more difficult. To pray well, to grow in the knowledge of God, we must pray; and to be able to pray well, we have to learn how to pray, to live through, perhaps, many years in which we seem to gain little fruit and are often scarcely conscious of any progress.

And, moreover, each has practically to learn for himself how to pray. We may gain some encouragement, some little help from others, but the real secret of prayer we must learn for ourselves. How can anyone teach another the form of conversation with a friend? It grows, unfolds, develops of itself; it is intensely personal.

We may learn something from the experience of others as to where dangers lie, as to possible self-deception, the need of perseverance through times of darkness and coldness; but the inmost secret of prayer must be our own. It is the deepest expression of the soul's personal relationship with God. It is, indeed, in one sense like, but in another unlike, the prayer of anyone else.

If God has given us any power in prayer, we shall find that it is impossible to communicate the secret of that power to anyone else; when we try to tell that, we fail. We may repeat the prayer that we say, and tell of some of the trials and struggles through which we have passed, but we cannot tell just that thing that gives the power and strength to our prayers, for, in fact, it is our relationship to God Himself; it is the expression of all that we mean by our spiritual life.

Yet there are certain dangers that are common to most people, and certain principles on which growth in the life of prayer must be based.

To many persons it seems, when first they begin in earnest the practice of prayer, that the best guide is their own devotion, that in spiritual matters system and rule crush out all spontaneity and life, and that often even the mere attitude of kneeling chills them and makes them formal. They find that they can pray better at work than on their knees, at irregular times of exceptional fervor than at stated times, and that consequently the best rule is to pray when they can pray best. Such persons have a proper dread of formalism, and it seems to them as if system and rule must degenerate into formalism if prayers are to be said at stated times whether there is any fervor of spirit or not. Yet such persons should remember:

• *As time goes on, those inspirations and times of fervor, unless carefully disciplined, become less frequent and intense, and at last probably die out altogether.* They belong to the early years of spiritual youth; they are given to help the soul in those first arduous struggles with bad habits and sins of the past, but they pass away; they are not a necessary part of the saintly life; they are, moreover, full of imperfections, and those who depend on such states of mind for prayer will find that, as time goes on, they pray less, not more.

• *Everything is of value only insofar as it helps to form character.* A person whose conversation with God depends mainly on the amount of emotional fervor he experiences will not have much strength of will or determination. The life of prayer cannot be built on anything so unreliable as feelings without being itself unreliable; it is built rather on acts of the will.

The religious character, therefore, is developed, and more is done for God by system and regularity than by all the fervor and excitement in the world. A great part of the discipline of faith is the holding on to God in darkness; one, therefore, who goes on regularly with prayer in coldness and deadness as faithfully as in times of the greatest fervor, thanking God when He makes His presence felt, but not laying too much stress on it, not gauging his progress by it, but believing that it is the will, fighting its way through darkness and almost the chill of death, that is accepted by God; such a person's character is altogether a more religious one and a stronger one than the other, and moreover we shall find that he has a far deeper and truer knowledge of God. The effort to get nearer God when He seems far off awakens a longing and strengthens the will in a way that one whose prayers depend on emotion can never experience.

The religious character that is ruled by impulse is quite a different one from that which is governed by principle. God can reveal Himself in darkness as well as in light: we are told that "clouds and darkness are round about him"[37] and that He

---

[37] Ps. 97:2.

"coverest himself with light as with a garment."[38] Those, therefore, who will not pray in darkness lose that special revelation that God gives through the darkness, and surely none who have persevered through such times can doubt that God revealed Himself to them then. When the darkness has passed, the soul will find what an increased knowledge and love of God it has gained.

• *Devotion is of two kinds, essential and accidental.* The word *devotion* means "consecration," which is an act of the will — offered, dedicated, devoted. Essential devotion, then, is devotion of the will offered to God and independent of any emotion. He who prays in such a spirit, offering himself to bear whatever God may send, is certainly devout, whatever he may feel, even though his whole time of prayer be spent in nothing but a struggle with distraction. God will not refuse to accept the service of a will that is devoted to Him.

Accidental devotion arises when there flows in upon the will that is thus holding on to God the light and joy and peace that stirs the heart and feelings. This is, after all, but accidental; it is not of the essence of devotion; one may be very devout without it. For the deepest love is the love that has passed down into the will and rules there.

The love that a young couple experience in the first days of their married life is full of passion and feeling; but after they have lived together for years and their lives are woven into one another, those passionate feelings of love have mostly given way to a stronger love that rules the will. They probably feel little of what they used to experience, but now each rules and

---

[38] Ps. 104:2.

molds the other's life. Perhaps it is only when there comes the possibility of a separation that either one realizes how intense their love is.

So it is in prayer. We must not gauge our devotion by what we feel, but rather by what we are ready to endure. Indeed, it often happens that God tries the most advanced by letting them experience a coldness and deadness in prayer such as ordinary people seldom experience, and none could endure in such times if their love for God were not very deep and strong, ruling and sustaining the will.

Now, in considering the act of prayer itself, we must remember that it is composed of a natural and a supernatural element: the act of the person who prays and the help that God gives. Different classes of minds are in danger of laying undue stress on one or the other of these parts as if it comprised the whole, but all true prayer involves both.

Therefore, due consideration must be given to both parts. If the best musician in the world were playing on an organ that was out of tune, he could not produce good music, and if the Holy Spirit were to breathe over our souls in prayer while the strings were lax from damp or carelessness, He could not produce the music that God loves to hear.

Our prayer may fail, therefore, not because God does not help us, but because we have not taken proper care in preparing ourselves; the strings of the mind are out of tune. We shall never get so high as to be able to leave out of consideration our own preparation and discipline. And, on the other hand, if the mind were under perfect control and discipline, we would never be able to pray without the help of God's Holy Spirit. The organ may be in perfect tune, but it needs the hand of the musician to draw out its powers.

When we come to our prayers, we must place ourselves beneath His influence. "The Spirit also helpeth our infirmities: for we know not what we should pray for as we ought."[39]

Let us consider these two elements then, the natural and the supernatural.

The Natural

The mind must be prepared.

So many of our prayers are poor and unworthy because the mind is not properly prepared; one kneels with the best disposition, but the mind has got into a morbid condition, and the whole time of prayer is lost in a kind of unhealthy self-examination; or it is absorbed in some matter that it has allowed to take possession of it, and the time is spent without ever rising to God. Or again, no sooner does one kneel than it seems to be the signal for the imagination to break loose and bring before the mind everything he has thought, said, or done, and everyone he has seen during the day.

It is important, therefore, that we should remember that the instrument with which we pray is that with which we do all our other mental work; when we turn it to God, we shall find that it has the same defects and the same powers that it has at other times, only that we become more conscious of the defects in times of prayer.

No wonder it is difficult to pray if there is no effort made to discipline or concentrate the mind at other times; how can the mind that is left relaxed and unguarded all through the day be recollected in prayer?

[39] Rom. 8:26.

Deepen Your Friendship with God

Prayer is not the only time to struggle against distractions; the more orderly, methodical, disciplined, and concentrated our minds are during our daily life, the more we shall be able to direct them to God in prayer.

There is nothing, therefore, that we do during the day that may not prove a help or hindrance in times of prayer. In reading, working, and thinking, we are unconsciously training our minds for prayer. If it is the same mind that we use for all our ordinary work that we use in prayer, the same and no other, we shall find the same laxity, the same distractedness, the same slipshod and careless ways, the same habit of losing ourselves in daydreams at prayer that we experience in all our mental life.

It is a good thing, therefore, to remember that prayer is not the time to train the mind, but that in prayer we shall reap the fruits of the carelessness or watchfulness of our ordinary life.

Prayer calls for common sense.
Again, it must be remembered that the mind is a very delicate instrument, and is very easily put out of order, and that spiritual work does not exempt people from natural laws. We need, therefore, care and common sense just as much in spiritual as in temporal things; a person may suffer very considerably in his spiritual life from lack of the exercise of a little common sense.

- *In learning to pray, it is therefore most important not to over-burden oneself at first with too many prayers.* Leave plenty of room to grow, be content at first to say such prayers as are suited to a beginner. If you would ever be able to spend a long time in prayer, you must begin with short times; the mind must be seasoned. Do not let prayer hang over you as a burden. It may be an admirable exercise in humility to confess to oneself how short a time one is able to pray; the mind must grow into the life of prayer, but it will never do this if it is allowed to be overweighed with a burden of prayer beyond its strength.

• *Again, do not leave your prayers to be said when the mind is too wearied to think.* If you are obliged to be up late, say the greater part of your prayers earlier in the evening. It is a fatal thing to go to one's room at night tired out and burdened with the dread of a considerable time to be spent in prayer, much of which, experience has taught, will be a mere struggle with sleep. One will never learn to pray by such methods; the mind needs in prayer the exercise of all its powers, and prayer should be said when the mind is fresh and in full vigor.

The times of prayer, therefore, should be arranged so that the natural instrument is at its best, not at its worst, and it should be always borne in mind that God does not give His grace to help us to do what nature can do of itself. You have no right to expect God to help you to say your prayers when you are tired, because you have not taken the trouble to say them in proper time.

• *There must be, if there is any life in prayer, adaptability.* One of the chief conditions of life is the capacity of adapting inward to outward relations. It is the same with prayer. Prayers in sickness will not be the same as in health if they are the utterances of a living soul: and in times of special trial or temptation, prayers will not be those of one's ordinary life. The soul, in proportion as prayer becomes a reality, will instinctively adapt its prayers to special circumstances, not indeed changing lightly the form of prayer, but having that liberty of spirit that makes a rule not a hindrance but a help, not the destroyer but the developer of life.

The Supernatural

But there is also the supernatural element in prayer. We must, indeed, discipline and train our minds, and fulfill our part; but prayer is not a mere straining of the mind toward God. We must pray as members of Christ: "He hath made us accepted in the beloved."[40]

We pray not as those who have nothing to depend on but their own efforts, but as those whose acceptance is already assured if they have faith to realize their great privileges. We Christians speak, as it were, with the lips of Christ. We know that in proportion as we believe in and use our great privilege, God cannot reject us.

Our own powers may be very limited, the sense of our sins may dismay us, but we draw near with the life of our Lord within us, "members of his body, of his flesh, and of his bones,"[41] and we know that God will hear the voice of His own Son.

Yet this sense of membership in Christ must be developed not merely at the times of prayer; it must be the effort of our daily life, the aim of our self-discipline. For it is on this that our Lord's promise depends: "If you abide in me, and my words abide in you, you shall ask what you will, and it shall be done unto you."[42] And as members of Christ we have the assistance

40 Eph. 1:6.
41 Eph. 5:30.
42 Cf. John 15:7.

of the Holy Spirit, "who helpeth our infirmities."[43] We kneel, but, notwithstanding all our watchfulness and care, our hearts are cold, and our words come falteringly; but we persevere, and then at times — not always consciously, but at times — we feel the breath of the Spirit breathing through us and kindling our devotion, and words come to our lips, or longings too great for words well up within our hearts and reach to God.

We feel, in one way, that what we say and long for is our own; it has the color and temper of our minds. But again we feel it is not our own; it is greater and stronger than we are. And then we know that it is partly ourselves, partly the Spirit of God — that the music that thrills us is the breath of the Spirit breathing through the instrument that we have striven so hard to prepare.

Such moments we must cherish and recall in times of darkness; they enable us to feel and to know that we are not alone in our efforts to pray, but that there is One who helps our infirmities, and who, when He sees fit, at any moment can make His power to be felt, even though when we are least conscious of it He is still with us.

[43] Rom. 8:26.

Chapter 7

⌒

Dwell in the Presence of God

The supreme work of life is the perfect development of character, having ever in view the will and purpose of God, the development of all that God has given us in relation to Himself, and the harmonizing of all the various gifts and powers with which we are endowed, so as to form one perfect whole. Each has to develop his own personal life and to resist all those manifold conflicting claims and forces that are constantly trying to interfere with it and to hurt it.

It is scarcely possible for anyone to live a single day without finding that someone or something has been intruding upon him in a way that, if he does not resist it, will more or less injure him.

Other lives and interests cross ours. We may allow ourselves to get entangled by a thousand claims and occupations that are not really any concern of ours. Things in which no duty compels us to interfere constantly press forward and solicit our interference. On all sides multitudes of things, sometimes the least trifles, sometimes matters of greater moment, seem arrayed against us, for no purpose apparently but to dissipate our powers and prevent the concentration and growth of our life. It is not, indeed, easy for the most conscientious always to know where to draw the line or to see what is an intrusion and what is a duty; when to hold aloof and let things of interest pass by and when to take part in them; what is the claim of charity and what is the mere fussiness of pride.

It is, therefore, of the utmost importance that we should know how to protect ourselves from all these distractions, and how to deal with the various circumstances with which we come in contact, in such a way as to force them to help and develop our true life, not to hinder it. There are, however, two dangers that we must be on our guard against, two wrong ways of meeting these difficulties.

Excessive Self-Consciousness

No one will ever develop his best self by always watching himself. There are some people who go through life wrapped in a kind of garment of spiritual self-consciousness. They never for a moment forget themselves and their own spiritual state; they are so afraid of being hurt by life, that, in their effort after self-protection, they inflict a fatal injury upon themselves that puts a stop to any healthy growth. They become morbid, introspective, timid, scrupulous; there is nothing spontaneous, nothing inspiring in their lives. They hold themselves back from all those experiences through which alone it is possible that life and character should develop, seeking to protect themselves sometimes at the expense of definite obligations. They fail to see that in neglecting to be responsive and sympathetic, they leave the richest side of their own nature stunted and maimed.

For God has so ordered it that our lives are bound up with one another, and in neglecting the claims of charity and the calls of duty we injure ourselves. All these duties and interests have their danger, no doubt, but in timidly shrinking from the dangers that duty involves, we fly into greater danger, for a life that has turned in upon itself and is always watching its own growth (or lack of growth) has already contracted a deadly disease. No, the atmosphere of spiritual self-consciousness and introspection is not the shelter that the soul is to find against the distracting interferences of life.

Undisciplined Freedom

But there is another danger. We must not, on the other hand, let ourselves go with undisciplined freedom. There are those who delight in feeling the play of life's many interests and sympathies upon them. With them there is no reserve, no self-restraint, but a constant outpouring of sympathy and activity. Rightly revolting against the narrow, inexpansive self-consciousness of some so-called religious people, they go to the other extreme and pour themselves out upon everyone and everything that interests them. Everything leaves its mark upon their impressionable natures. Finally, we feel that it needs only time and sufficiently strong influences to destroy every marked token of individuality in such people and to exhaust all the gifts with which they began life.

Character certainly does not ripen to its perfection in an atmosphere of general benevolence and undisciplined sympathy, nor will the soul find its shelter in such a self-forgetfulness as that.

Finding a Balance

Shall we, then, tell the former class of persons that they must get out of themselves by throwing themselves in a spirit of self-abandonment into the lives and interests of others, and the latter that they must hold themselves back and check the outgoings of their sympathy and try to harden themselves against that sensitive appreciation that exposes them to so much danger? Undoubtedly they must do this to a certain extent, but they will not find in such an endeavor the real remedy for their fault.

No, there is a better way: let each try to live in that atmosphere that will at once protect and develop his life, enabling him to keep the balance between the twofold claim from within and from without, yielding himself to the circumstances and influences that demand his sympathy, yet never losing hold of himself, and living the inner life without self-contemplation or the fear to go forth wherever and whenever duty calls.

The earth in its orbit around the sun passes through many thousands of miles, yet those who live on it are not conscious of any sudden and great changes, for it bears its own atmosphere about with it. And as we pass from one place and occupation to another, we need to carry our own atmosphere with us to protect and develop our lives.

How shall we do this?

What kind of atmosphere should we be wrapped in? How shall we pass from prayer to pleasure, from silence into crowded places, without jar or loss? How shall we practice watchfulness without becoming morbidly introspective? How shall we sustain large-hearted and generous charity, and sensitiveness that both feels and begets sympathy, without wasting ourselves? How shall we be able constantly "to go in and out and find pasture"[44] to shelter ourselves from the rude intrusions that would spoil our lives and yet never fail to go forth with our whole nature alive to every proper claim of the ever-widening world that asks our help.

[44] John 10:9.

Dwell in the Presence of God

There is one sure way: by living more and more in that atmosphere that draws out all the powers of the soul, that necessitates its growth, and in which at the same time it finds protection from every breath that would blight or stunt it, that intensifies all its sympathies and enables it to see all things in their true proportion.

And that atmosphere is the presence of God.

The soul that has learned to shelter itself in that presence has gained the protection it needs, from itself on the one hand, and, on the other, from the crowding appeals of life. In that presence there can be no morbidness, for it is the very truth; no stagnation, for it is the fountain of life; no timid holding back from the true claims of life, for that presence itself bids the soul go forth to work and action.

Nor, on the other hand, can one who lives in that presence fritter away his life upon things that have no claim upon him, for it ever holds back as well as sends forward.

He who lives beneath its shelter knows full well that the light and protection is limited to the sphere of duty and right, and that if he goes beyond that, he must leave it; but within that sphere he is safe amidst all the noise and distraction and wearying strain of life. "Thou art my hiding place; thou shalt preserve me from trouble; thou shalt compass me about with songs of deliverance."[45] "Thou shalt hide them in the secret of thy presence from the pride of man: thou shalt keep them secretly in a pavilion from the strife of tongues."[46]

In proportion as we gain the sense of God's presence, we are safe in the very tumult of life, in the very thick of the strife

[45] Ps. 32:7.
[46] Ps. 31:20.

of tongues. For this presence protects our own individuality; it protects us so that we do not lose ourselves, and become, as we are often apt to do, almost a mechanical part of the world and the society in which we live, sinking into a routine in which we lose more and more the sense of responsibility.

We certainly need this, a clear and ever-deepening sense of our own separate and solitary individuality, with all its consciousness of personal responsibility and the dignity of personal life. And the first thing that the realization of God's presence does for any man is to deepen this sense of his own personality and responsibility. He lives in a presence that is stronger than all the influences around him; that presence isolates him, frees him from the tyranny of the standards and judgments of the little coteries that make his world, and gives him new standards to judge himself by.

Many of those who have the capacities for influencing others, if only they could stand a little apart and be firm, are simply carried hither and thither by the babel of opinion in which they live and give themselves no time to pause and ask what it is all worth and what is their own duty. They have formed no clear idea of themselves, no notion of something definite that they were intended to be and to do. Having no strong convictions, they are borne hither and thither by the society in which they may happen to be for the moment.

And when such a person wakens to realize the presence of God, instantly there follows the quickened sense of his own personality and responsibility; he is wrapped around and stands alone in the presence that forces him to pass judgment upon himself. He sees himself in the presence of One who knows him and has been the silent witness of all he has ever said or done; he is compelled to gather himself out of the multitude, and the full recognition of his own personal responsibility is forced upon him.

Dwell in the Presence of God

There has come upon him something stronger than any of those influences that hitherto have acted upon him, robbing him almost of all sense of personality, and now he is able to stand alone and to withstand what before seemed impossible. "Thou art my hiding place.... Thou shalt compass me about with songs of deliverance."

There is something very wonderful in the way in which the thought of God at once wakens the dormant or half-lost sense of one's own personality and the responsibilities that it involves. We cannot come near Him without realizing ourselves more deeply. When Isaiah saw His glory, his first words were, "Woe is me, for I am undone, because I am a man of unclean lips ... for mine eyes have seen the King, the LORD of hosts!"[47] Made as we are in the image of God, there is an instinctive rising to compare ourselves to Him who is the source of our life and our Archetype.

This realization of God's presence is the power that gives such an intense personality to many who naturally would not be strong enough to stand alone. Encircled by this presence, they present that wonderful combination of sensitive timidity and moral courage that belongs to the Christian alone. This is the way of men and women who are not by nature strong or independent, but who cling much to others and depend much on others' judgment, yet when occasion demands are able quietly to go and do their work in the face of adverse criticism and misunderstanding, for their lives are strong and self-possessed, living in the presence of Him to whom they are responsible. Amidst all the pain that they may have to suffer, they verily have a "joy which no man taketh from them."[48]

[47] Isa. 6:5.
[48] Cf. John 16:22.

The presence of God is thus a shelter and protection for those whose duties compel them to live amidst many distractions and much variety of circumstances. It is as when one goes into a crowded room, and on all sides one hears a babel of voices and sees a multitude of people, one feels oneself lost in the presence of so many; and there amongst them you see one who is very dear to you, and as you draw near to him and hear his voice it seems as if you were leaving all that noisy crowd in the distance, and the tones of his voice at last so absorb you that they silence all else, and the tumult has ceased, and you and he are alone.

"Thou shalt keep them secretly in a pavilion from the strife of tongues"; and this the presence of God can do for us. We can withdraw ourselves at any moment when we feel ourselves getting lost, as it were, in a crowded life, and rest under the shelter of His presence.

In this way we may protect our life from dissipating its powers and from losing itself amidst the distractions into which duty or pleasure may call us. "The name of the Lord is a strong tower: the righteous runneth into it and is safe."[49]

But, on the other hand, the practice of the presence of God will be the remedy for those whose danger is to hold aloof from duties and to become spiritually self-centered. For the presence of God at once lifts one out of oneself, yet not in such a way as to leave one in ignorance of one's faults; one sees oneself — indeed, one knows oneself — in a far truer way than by any amount of introspection, but one sees oneself without self-contemplation and without self-depreciation.

Living in a constant spirit of self-watching and self-analysis, one may be quite possibly measuring himself by false standards;

---

[49] Prov. 18:10.

perhaps by the ideal that his own pride has drawn for him, perhaps by the standard of some other's life, he may be striving
after what God never meant and never gave him the power to
attain. But as we learn to live in the presence of God, all this
becomes impossible. In the presence of the truth, we are forced
to be true, and it is astonishing to see how those whose aims
were very lofty and very unreal, and who had gotten into an
altogether false method of weighing the value of spiritual things,
gradually, as they strove to live more in God's presence, took a
wholly different and truer estimate of life and thought less and
talked less about their own spiritual life. "Thou requirest truth
in the inward parts, and shalt make me to understand wisdom
secretly."[50] They unconsciously gained another standard as they
lived more simply before God. They grew out of a timid life of
self-analysis into a strong life in which they saw themselves as
God would have them to be. Yet their self-knowledge became,
in fact, far deeper and truer.

Certainly, if we need protection from life's many distractions
and calls, we need perhaps even more protection from that ever-
present atmosphere of self-consciousness that clings to so many
like a damp fog; and, not by any means, the least dangerous form
is spiritual self-consciousness. And we cannot get out of this by
merely struggling with it, as we might struggle with temper or
pride; such efforts seem often only to rivet the bonds more tightly
upon us. We can get out of it only by losing ourselves in another,
and there is but One other whose presence we can always have,
who will never weary us, and who will never harm us.

But we must not expect that we shall be able to gain such a
protecting sense of God's presence in a moment. It will be the

[50] Cf. Ps. 51:6.

result of much prayer and mental discipline. We must not be discouraged, therefore, if after a long time we still find that we have made but little progress.

"In his presence is the fullness of joy; and at his right hand there is pleasure for evermore."[51] The fullness of joy and such lasting pleasure are not to be easily gained; they are to be won only by those who work hard and suffer much for it.

A few suggestions may be helpful to those who are beginning the practice of the presence of God.

- *The mind must be kept in a healthy state*; if it becomes over-strained, it will never be able to attain to the power of resting in God's presence. The realizing of the presence of God is not to be accomplished by a straining of the mind or by a forcing of the imagination; the soul must grow into it gradually; it must be a rest, not a weariness. Therefore, anytime the mind feels strained or wearied, it should be relaxed; we should turn to something else and give it rest.

  We may test our progress by the growing sense of liberty, the facility and freedom from scruple or anxiety with which the mind rests itself when it feels the danger of strain or weariness; scruple and fear and a burden of rules will make advance in this practice impossible.

- *Do not be anxious to grow too fast.* If you are impatient and overtax your strength, you will fail altogether. To live in God's presence means to be very holy, and, therefore, to grow in the sense of His presence means growth in holiness. It is one of the chief fruits of a holy life,

---

[51] Cf. Ps. 16:11.

and we cannot see that fruit except as the life grows and deepens. One part, so to speak, of the spiritual life cannot outstrip all the rest; be patient, therefore, and be content to grow slowly. It is good, indeed, never to forget the presence of God for a moment, but it would be fatal to begin by even trying to keep the mind always concentrated. "When I was a child I thought as a child."[52] Begin by recalling the thought of God's presence at certain times, by setting apart a few minutes once or twice in the day to remain quietly wrapping yourself around with the thought, and be content with this until you are spiritually ready for more. The evil results of lack of prudence, which is often lack of humility, will not be healed by grace.

* *In work that should occupy the mind, give your mind to it.* Offer it to God when you begin and when you finish it. But while at work you must seek to glorify God by using all the powers of your mind in what you are doing. Therefore, do not try to realize God's presence at such times, except during in a moment's pause, but let the conscious thought of His glory stimulate you to do your best.

* *Build the practice of the presence of God upon the indwelling presence of Christ.*[53] Let each Communion remind you of what you are as a Christian — a member of Christ, fed by His life. Let each Communion intensify the realization of that ever-abiding presence within you, and

---

[52] Cf. 1 Cor. 13:11.
[53] See Gal. 2:20.

let the thought of each Communion remain with you until your next, even if through no fault of yours a long period intervenes. Some may seek to place themselves in the presence of God as in an atmosphere of holy light wrapping around them — that luminous "shadow of the Almighty"[54] of which the psalmist speaks. But it will be perhaps an easier, certainly a surer and a quicker road to holiness to turn within and to rest oneself upon that heavenly light that burns in the inmost depth of the soul, radiating forth upon all its powers and faculties, the Shekinah of the divine presence.[55] "In the secret place of His dwelling shall He hide me, and set me up upon a rock of stone."[56]

---

[54] Ps. 91:1.

[55] *Shekinah* refers to "the dwelling place of God. It is any visible manifestation of God's presence, several times alluded to in the Bible. It corresponds to God's glory in Isaiah 60:2, his glory in Romans 9:4, and the cloud that directed the Israelites on their way to the Promised Land (Exodus 14:19)." Fr. John Hardon, S.J., *Modern Catholic Dictionary*, s.v. "Shekina," http://www.therealpresence.org/dictionary/adict.htm.

[56] Cf. Ps. 27:5.

Chapter 8

Enter into Your Hidden Life

There were two sides to the life of our Lord. To those who saw Him in His public ministry during the last three years of His life, it seemed one of constant and unceasing labor. He "went about doing good."[57] He was ever at the call of any who needed Him; He gave Himself no rest, so that He had not so much time as to eat bread. In the Gospels, we read of days crowded with work of the most trying kind, dealing constantly with all sorts of people, addressing crowds and then meeting the needs of individuals, and never apparently alone, the Apostles always with Him. His life was almost lived in public; almost the whole Gospel is taken up with the events of about three years. To those who saw Him and heard Him, it was as if His life seemed to be without rest, a life of unsparing energy and toil.

But there was another side that they could not see — the hidden life. His public life was built upon and rested upon a life of thirty years of hiddenness and preparation. For every year in public there were ten years in private. In the solitude and

[57] Acts 10:38.

retirement of Nazareth He grew up; there His human character formed and developed, far from the noise and excitement of the world. Thirty years out of thirty-three He lived there, almost His whole life. What does three years count for in many a man's life? And He spent His whole life except three years at Nazareth.

And even after that long period of preparation, He retired into deeper solitude before His public ministry began. He spent forty days in the wilderness in absolute solitude, except for the presence of visitors from the world of spirits. And again and again we read of His withdrawing in the midst of His life of active work for prayer. "In the morning, rising up a great while before day, he went out and departed into a solitary place, and there prayed."[58]

Yes, there was the hidden life from which the public life gained all its power. All His actions were rooted in God; He never forgot Himself, never got carried away by the interest or excitement of the multitudes with whom He had to deal, never swerved from the purpose and will of God.

The hidden life *is* hidden; we know almost nothing about it. If it were known and could be described, it would not be hidden. Now and again, in the thick and pressure of His work, the veil is lifted for a moment, and we are allowed to see those nights of prayer. Men could feel and see the mysterious power in His words and acts and bearing that were the outward manifestations of that inner life, but that was all. His life — that out of which all this public life grew — was hidden.

It is the same with the Body of Christ — the Church. She has her public life; we read of it in history; we see it today. The

[58] Mark 1:35.

Church, everywhere in all the world's busiest places, teaching, mingling with all the thought and interests of the day, struggling against opposition, dealing with sin and suffering and misery, never resting, pressing forward into new fields of conquest, beset with temporal needs that have to be met.

How is she to live and grow in such scenes? How, amidst the strain and pressure that is upon her on all sides, is she to keep true to God?

There are so many inducements to compromise and to advance by worldly methods; so little time to collect herself and to meet the requirements of a new age. What is to support her? What gives her that power so far beyond her number and the influence of her individual members? The Church, too, must have her hidden life upon which she rests, from which she draws her succors, by which she preserves her strength.

She is now, like our Lord, in her public life pressed and driven and beset, like Him, by the needy multitude and by her many antagonists. But her life is not merely what is seen and heard: the Church has another life that cannot be seen nor measured, but on which she depends for all her power, from which she draws all the secret of her strange influence. The Church, if she is to live, must have her hidden life of prayer and fasting and solitude.

The Church is one Body composed of many members. All men are bound to one another by the tie of a common nature, but Christians are bound by a twofold tie, the tie of a common nature and of membership in Christ: "For by one Spirit are we all baptized into one body."[59] And it follows that the Church

---

[59] 1 Cor. 12:13.

can live one part of her life through some of her members and another part through others, for so closely are all the members bound together in one Body that, as St. Paul says, "if one member suffer, all the members suffer with it; or one member be honored, all the members rejoice with it."[60]

Therefore, as the different members of the body have their different functions and work for the edification of the body, so in the Body of Christ all have not the same office; there is a division of labor amongst the members, but it is for the life of the Body. Thus the Church goes forth into the world through some; through others she keeps up that hidden life which is her strength. The work of some is seen and heard and attracts notice; it is done, as our Lord's works in His ministry were done, before the world. The work of others is not seen; it is only felt.

Just as in the natural body we can see a man working and hear him speak, but we cannot see the processes by which the body is nourished and life preserved, for all the work of preserving and strengthening the life is unseen, so, in the Body of Christ, the development of its inner strength, the preservation and growth of its life, is hidden. Behind all the movements of its activity is the hidden life from which it draws its power. "Are all apostles? Are all prophets? Are all teachers?... Do all speak with tongues?"[61]

There are all over the world, many, of whom men know little or nothing, who are the fountains of the Church's strength. How strange they are, those lives of constant suffering: men and women who seem cast aside and useless, tied down to sickbeds, it may be with bodies paralyzed or enfeebled so that they cannot

---

[60] 1 Cor. 12:26.
[61] 1 Cor. 12:29, 30.

work; souls struck down in their prime and doomed to years of lingering illness and wasting strength. What use can such lives be except to try the patience of those who have to tend them? But no; they little know themselves that it is upon such lives as theirs that the Church depends for power to bear up against the world and to prosecute her missionary labors. If, on one side, there is a great putting forth of strength, there must be on the other a proportionate building up and nourishment, or the life will be soon exhausted.

So, in one way or another, God will surely call people to the life of retirement and prayer or suffering in proportion as the demands upon the Church become more exacting. The call may take many forms, and perhaps different forms in different ages, but such calls are surely given.

Sometimes it may be in a most unobtrusive way. A person is kept back time after time from the opportunity of doing active work. How often has a young woman in her own home looked forward to devoting herself to some work. Perhaps she has had it in her mind for years and believed God was calling her to it; but every time, just as the opportunity seemed to come, the door was closed in her face: some clear call of duty, sickness, the care of those who depended on her—one thing or another always blocked the way and threw her back.

It seemed to her a puzzle that God should appear to call and not give the power to correspond; but it may be, although she felt the call, she mistook its meaning, and God was leading her on unconsciously to fulfill it. She was thrown back upon prayer; her longing to help others needed some vent, and she found it in intercession; then she passed on from intercessory prayers to intercessory acts, until her life was one of constant sacrifice for those whom she was apparently held back from helping. Her vocation was to the hidden life; no one ever noticed it, least of all herself. For her life was "hidden with Christ in God."[62]

Or it may be a priest, full of zeal for souls, and with great missionary gifts, struck down a few years after his ordination, and, as people said, a most promising and useful life put an end to. And yet, as years went by, those who knew him best saw another life grow and spring up amidst the ruins of the old one, as one sees the bud form under the dead leaf of autumn. None of the zeal had been lost, none of the love for souls, none of the sacerdotal spirit, but it had been purified and redirected into the offering of a better sacrifice than service, the sacrifice of himself. He had grasped more and more the mystery of vicarious suffering, and his life went up in one unending sacrifice and oblation for those whom in act he was prevented from helping.

Or again, that multitude of lives, in no way marked, that as time goes on get mellowed and softened by age, and perhaps by the ordinary disappointments of life, from whom most of the world's attraction has long since passed, and in their place has come a growing love of God and a desire to do something for others before they die to atone for a selfish, aimless life. From how many such lives there goes up before God a constant stream of prayer and acts, many of them enforced acts of self-denial, and often intense inward suffering borne with fortitude and in silence. The world has gone from them and heaven has not come; the remnants of old worldly ways, which they hate, still cling to them, causing them bitter humiliations.

Their place in very truth knows them no more, and still with all there is a pathetic effort to lay hold on God with minds dulled and heavy, and to keep up their interest in the world by praying

[62] Cf. Col. 3:3.

for it. Surely such lives have power, and such prayers, joyless strugglings after an unseen God, are not rejected; and truly such lives are hidden, for few are sufficiently interested in them to remark them.

But, above all, the hidden life of the Church is to be found in the cloister, amongst those whose vocation is primarily — in many cases, only — to a life of prayer. Behind all the active life of the Church stand those great religious orders devoted to prayer and penitence, witnessing to the world that Christianity is not merely a philanthropic society, but that it is devotion to a Person.

These men and women devote themselves not to active work for their brethren — in many cases, they shut themselves out from the possibility of any such work — but believing that the closer they are to God, the more real help they can bring to the world, they give up everything else that they may draw ever closer to Him.

As they approach Him, and their lives are more united to Him, their sympathies become enlarged, for their hearts are close to the Heart of the world's Redeemer. All interests but His die out, but all that is dear to Him becomes the absorbing passion of their souls. They are able to enter as few others into His sympathies, to long with His longing for the salvation of souls, to enter with opening vision into the mystery of the Atonement and Redemption till they yearn to partake to some measure in His sufferings, to suffer with Him for others' sins. They realize something of the reality of the unity of the Body of Christ and of the power of vicarious suffering.

Who can tell of the power that from age to age has gone forth from these unknown lives? — men and women literally buried out of the world's sight and knowledge, who, while the world has gone on its way and enjoyed itself, and often sneered at the selfish lives of those who fled from it to save their own souls, little knew that they were the world's saviors, whose lives are a living sacrifice for their brethren.

Yes, the Church has her hidden life, the secret of her power, the unseen fountains of her strength. If the Church's life were only what men gauged it by and applauded it for — what they could see and measure by results gained and assured — if that were all, that must soon exhaust itself and fail. But there is another side, its true strength, which many count as waste of strength, "all that the world's coarse thumb and finger cannot plumb,"[63] the life hidden with Christ in God.

And as with our Lord and His Body, so with the individual soul. Everyone has the outer life and the inner life, the life that is lived before the world and the life that none can see but God. To some the outer life is the main thing; they think little of the hidden life; they would gladly not think of it at all.

To others the hidden life is the first, the chief consideration of all; it is that for which they live; it is from its springs that they draw their strength; it is for its sake that the most real sacrifices are made. Yet the most hopelessly superficial person has his hidden life — that inner life of compromises with conscience, of breaking down barriers that God has set up between the soul and sin, of secrets that it has with itself, that none shall ever know of, things done that it will not allow even itself to face and to acknowledge; of memories driven off into dark corners of the soul that come out at night like ghosts and haunt it; of a deepening sense of dissatisfaction and of unfulfilled possibilities — of a noble ideal of life that once was possible but now only returns to waken remorse and bitterness.

[63] From Robert Browning, *Rabbi Ben Ezra*.

Enter into Your Hidden Life

And then there is the growing feeling that always comes to such people sooner or later, that matters are passing out of their own hands, that currents are setting in one direction so fast that they cannot be controlled, that life has taken things into its own hands since the will has not taken the trouble to control them, and that all real liberty is gone.

Yes, the most superficial, the most utterly frivolous person, who seems to have no higher thought than the enjoyment of the moment's pleasure, has a hidden life, and I do not think it would be true to call it shallow; it has, indeed, an infinite depth; it is the beginning of the thirst that shall never be quenched.

Such is possibly the inner state of many who do not cultivate the hidden life, for it needs to be cultivated. The tendency of most natures is to begin by turning outward. The life of the infant begins with the senses; the claims of duty constantly call us out; the pressure of the outer life is enormous. A firm exercise of the will is needed to call the soul back into itself, that it may dwell within rather than without. It has but to let itself go, to take no trouble with itself, to practice no self-discipline, and it will drift further and further into the life of the senses, and get ever more entangled in external things.

But the true hidden life is not a mere holding back of the powers of the soul. No life is mere repression. It is possible to have one's life turned inward to its own destruction. There is the danger of self-absorption and self-contemplation that has to be constantly guarded against, for a soul whose inner life is merely or mostly self-contemplation is in a far worse state than one that lives a wholly external life. The hidden life is not to be a life of self-analysis and self-torturing, but the very reverse — it is to be a life that is deeply interior, yet with an entire self-forgetfulness.

What, then, is the source and meaning of the hidden life of the Christian? It is based upon those words of St. Paul, "I live, yet not I, but Christ liveth in me";[64] "Christ, in you the hope of glory."[65] It is rooted in the soul's union with Christ. It grows out of the fact that in baptism we are made "members of his Body,"[66] that "all our fresh springs henceforth are to be in Him."[67]

The soul that is striving to develop the hidden life turns inward — not in self-contemplation but to contemplate and to develop its union with Christ. It carries this sacred presence with it wherever it goes; it becomes increasingly conscious of a power within that is not its own, yet that is wholly at its disposal. It feels a growing strength, not the strength of its own natural gifts, but quite apart from all that it has naturally. It understands the meaning of St. Paul's paradox, "When I am weak, then am I strong."[68] It perceives its own weakness only too clearly, but it finds a power not its own that flows into it as it throws itself more and more upon the indwelling presence of Christ.

This presence, then, within each baptized Christian, is the source of its hidden life. Upon this it is built; the practice of the hidden life depends on the development of all that results from it, the using of the powers that flow from it. For although we have, every one of us, this great gift, its action depends on our faith and on our will. To many it is but a treasure hidden in the field; they weary themselves in the plowing and harrowing and sowing upon the surface of their nature, while the true source of their riches lies buried deep down within them.

[64] Gal. 2:20.
[65] Col. 1:27.
[66] Eph. 5:30.
[67] Cf. Ps. 87:7.
[68] 2 Cor. 12:10.

Enter into Your Hidden Life

If we would avoid the danger, on the one hand, of living wholly external lives and wasting our strength and, on the other hand, of becoming self-centered or morbidly introspective, we must strive to live the hidden life, to find the roots of our life running down into His, from whom comes our strength. All that helps toward this will be in the end a blessing.

Temptations that we have fought and failed to overcome for years may at last drive us to the one true source of power, drive us into ourselves to seek the power hidden there. Prayers that never seem to bring us nearer to God may at last lead us, if I may use such an expression, not so much to pray ourselves as to be silent and listen to Christ praying within us.

The hopelessness that comes from the memory of past sins and wasted years and gifts undeveloped may drive us, not to look to a Mediator upon the throne of God merely, but to the realization that we need more, more than One standing at God's right hand to intercede for us — even the presence of that mediatorial life within ourselves, our own living membership in Him who is the Mediator.

Yes, and if God is merciful to us, we shall feel the spring and movements of that new life amidst the decay and death of the old, rising like a fountain and fertilizing the barren soil, and making the wilderness to blossom as the rose. Out of the despair of nature will spring the dawn of the hope of grace; out of weakness strength.

This is the secret of the saints; this was the source of their power; this it was that puzzled men as they watched them: they could not see the source of that strength by which these saints were enabled to overcome the world, so far in excess of their natural gifts was their power, for their life was "hidden with Christ in God."

Chapter 9

⌒

Abide in Christ

The whole Christian life may be summed up in two acts—coming to Christ and abiding in Christ.

Coming to Christ

Everyone who has lost his baptismal innocence, if he will save his soul, has to come back to our Lord. Each has his own history, his own experience of all that this means. God leads different souls in different ways; some, no doubt, have stopped suddenly in a life of alienation and in a moment have turned and begun to trace their steps back; with others the process has been so slow and gradual that they can scarcely tell where or how it began. There was a growing discontent with their life, a deepening desire for better things, struggles often—most often—ending in failure, efforts to pray, a sense of weakness and of sin, a gradual movement accompanied by many relapses, that ended in the soul's finding itself turned and facing Godward.

Some have felt sensibly in all this process a marked and conscious action of God's grace, a sense of the divine assistance that at times seemed almost irresistible, making everything easy, and seeming to lift the soul out of the reach of its old temptations and habits. With others it has been different; there has been from moment to moment little sense of God's assistance or of His love, only the consciousness of the hand-to-hand struggle with sin and of the difficulties to be overcome. The experience of one is not the experience of another. God delights to deal with each in His own way as He sees to be best, and much harm is done by pressing personal experience into the sphere of dogma and trying to urge our own experiences upon others. It is only as they look back, it may be after many years, that they are able to say, "If the Lord Himself had not been on our side, when men rose up against us, they had swallowed us up quick, when they were so wrathfully displeased at us; but praised be the Lord, who hath not given us over for a prey unto their teeth: our soul is escaped, even as a bird out of the snare of the fowler; the snare is broken and we are delivered."[69]

There are two sides to all the actions of our Christian life — the work of our will and of the grace of God. God cannot work in us apart from our cooperation and all our most strenuous endeavors must fail without the assistance of His grace. Some are more conscious of one side, some of the other, although in all both the human and the divine must cooperate. St. Paul brings the two sides together when he says, "Work out your own salvation … for it is God that worketh in you."[70]

Our Lord teaches both sides when He says, "No man cometh unto me except the Father who hath sent me draw him";[71] and

[69] Cf. Ps. 124.
[70] Cf. Phil. 2:12–13.
[71] Cf. John 6:44.

again, "I, if I be lifted up, will draw all men unto me."[72] Here He teaches us the action of God upon the soul, but He says again, "Come unto me, all ye that labor and are heavy laden, and I will give you rest."[73] Here He appeals to the soul; the coming must be its own act. It is not to be wondered at that some ardent natures are most conscious of the drawing, while others feel most the action of their own will; the experiences of both are true to the teaching of Scripture, but each has felt one side so strongly that he has not been always conscious of the other.

Now, the coming to Christ is by a movement not of the body but of the mind; it is the entering into a certain relationship with a Person. We know how quickly we may travel away from one whom we have loved; it is not so easy to return. Not many days after the prodigal's breach with his father, he was in a far country; it took him a long time to get back. Two persons may be living side by side and gradually drifting further apart even though they are constantly in one another's company. A husband and wife, bound by God in that mystical union that makes the two "to be one flesh"[74] may nevertheless be as far apart as the poles. Two friends who had no interest apart one from the other a few days ago may find that some little jar or slight misunderstanding makes it impossible to give or take sympathy today; the voice that was so full of kindness seems to have lost its true ring. A separation has begun. Often, indeed, the closer and more intimate the friendship, the quicker and more complete the separation when once it begins; it is easier to make up a quarrel with a mere acquaintance than with a dear friend.

[72] John 12:32.
[73] Matt. 11:28.
[74] Mark 10:8.

Thus, there are constant movements of the heart and mind without any bodily movements; in a day, in an hour, the heart and mind and will may have gone a long journey. The drawing near of two friends or their separation is like nothing else. It is the mysterious action of one person upon another. How different it is from a merely intellectual process. You have read and inquired as much as possible about some well-known person; you know what he has done and said, and to a large extent you can understand the tone of his mind on most subjects, and you have made up your mind about him—you do not like him.

Yet five minutes in his company changes your whole feeling toward him; you have come directly in contact with his person and through a hundred channels he lets in upon you a knowledge of himself that you never could gain in any other way. You ask yourself what has made you change your mind. Has he argued away your prejudice? Has he answered the objections you had to his conduct? No, he has not even referred to them.

The fact is, you had previously only an intellectual knowledge *about* him; now you know him *himself*. That subtle thing, a personal life, has flowed in upon you through not one channel but many, and the conclusions of one part of your nature are corrected or balanced by those of another. What a journey you have taken in those five minutes from the time when you held aloof from him on your first meeting to the time—a few minutes after—when you felt prejudice, dislike, and antagonism all give way and you let yourself go out toward him, saying, "I like him." This is the coming of one person to another, the personal drawing near, not of the body but of the self.

And this is but an illustration of the soul's coming to Christ; it is the coming to a Person in such a way as only one person can come to another, the bringing oneself under and surrendering oneself to a personal influence. It does not consist in a great deal of knowledge *about* Him, but in knowing Him. Indeed, many have come to Him knowing very little about Him, learning all that was to be known from Himself. Nathanael came full of prejudice and with strong biblical arguments against what Philip had told him of His claims. Two sentences from our Lord's own lips sweep away all the arguments and prejudices, and bring him to His feet with a profession of faith like St. Peter's: "Thou art the Son of God; Thou art the king of Israel."[75]

In the formation of any friendship, two persons have to be considered; there may be obstacles or lack of sympathy or misunderstanding on both sides, or one may be most anxious for a friendship from which the other holds back. The friendship does not depend merely on the efforts of one.

But in drawing near to Christ, we know that there are no obstacles on His side. No, He does not have to be won over: He is the suppliant. The hindrances, prejudice, dislike, and ignorance are all on our side. If only we remove them, we shall find how close He is to us. We have taken our journey into a far country of moral alienation; we care for, are interested in, perhaps live wholly absorbed in things that are hateful to Him; and we are injuring the work for which He gave His life. However near we may be to Him outwardly, we are worlds apart from Him in heart and will, and the return must be by our effort to get into moral sympathy, our struggle to do right, and our determination at any rate to be in earnest.

He who longs and strives to be good has already created a bond of sympathy with Christ, has returned, indeed, a long way toward Him. As one after another of those barriers that we have

---

[75] John 1:49.

set up in ourselves are removed, light and love come streaming in, and the bonds of that mystical friendship become woven, to grow stronger through eternity.

It is a wonderful experience that the soul gains in the journey that consists not in traversing space, but in a moral approach, a turning of the mind to *contemplate* and of the will to *choose* and, at last, of the heart to *love* what Christ loves, and then finding behind all this the living, loving Person who reveals Himself.

The first act of the soul, then, is the coming to Christ; though this in one sense never ends, for it is ever drawing nearer as it grows in holiness and admits more and more of His knowledge and love.

Abiding in Christ

The other act is the abiding in Him. Having drawn near, it must abide. But it is always more difficult to be passive than to be active. The very effort in coming, the consciousness of meeting and overcoming difficulties, strengthens and encourages the soul; but to abide—that is where so many fail. Many of those who have drawn near turn aside and walk no more with Him—unable to persevere. Only he who is "faithful unto death shall receive the crown of life."[76] The life of the saints in heaven is the eternal abiding in Him to whom they came here on earth. Now the abiding in Christ involves three things.

Give up whatever hinders union with Christ.
First, negatively, abiding in Christ involves the giving up of everything that hinders this union. After the first great surrender

[76] Cf. Rev. 2:10.

of what is positively sinful, no rule can be laid down that is applicable to everyone. There are many things that are harmless in themselves that some feel obliged to give up if they would abide in Christ. There are things, indeed, that may be helpful to one that would be a hindrance to another. We cannot lay down arbitrary rules as to what is necessary to be given up in the way of pleasure or relaxation or self-indulgence. The wisest guide will, I believe, leave each to take the initiative as to what he must and must not do. It would be a fatal thing to begin by exacting too much. Who can tell how God intends to lead another?

All that the wisest can do is to point out what seems to be God's leading. The fact that I feel obliged to deal very sternly with myself does not necessarily mean that another should deal with himself likewise. A pleasure that would be wrong for me might be very good for another. Many a person might say with perfect truth, "I cannot give up such-and-such a thing; I do not love God sufficiently to do without it; my life would be too empty; it does not in any way come between me and God at present."

No, in the earlier stages of the spiritual life, it would not be true to say that God was all in all to one: there are doubtless various portions of one's life that God has not yet won to Himself, and these are filled up by pursuits and interests that, so far, do not interfere with God's hold upon the soul. The soul, so far as it knows God, is abiding in Him.

There is a better way of leading men onward; it is the way of nature as well as the way of grace—positively rather than negatively. I ask you as you begin to serve God to make but one rule: to give up all that you are conscious of hindering your union with Him. As you get to know Him better, He will become more exacting in His demands; you will find that many things that now are harmless and in a measure necessary to you will begin to interfere with your union with God. Resolve that if you find this, you will give them up.

You will be able to do in a few years what it would be absurd to ask you to do now. As God comes more into your life and demands that it should be more emptied of other things, obey Him, and He will reward you by a greater gift of Himself. The whole pathway of your life will thus be strewn with various things that you have abandoned for what is better, things that once seemed to you necessary to your life. The advance is a constant self-emptying, but not that your life may be a void, but to make room for larger interests, keener pleasures, deeper joys, a more absorbing love.

Once you said, "If the spiritual life means the giving up of this work or companionship, I do not think it would be worth the sacrifice."

"Very well," was the answer; "do not give it up. Keep it until you feel that the spiritual life is the love of a Person for whom it is worth giving it up."

Now it is gone, for you have come in sight of what is more worth having. The growth in the spiritual life is thus a constant exchange: first the giving up of what is positively bad for good, then the surrender of things good in themselves for better: "For brass I will bring gold, and for iron I will bring silver, and for wood brass, and for stones iron."[77] Such is the promise in the kingdom of the Messiah, and at last "the sun shall be no more thy light by day, neither for brightness shall the moon give light unto thee; but the LORD shall be unto thee an everlasting light, and thy God thy glory."[78]

[77] Isa. 60:17.
[78] Isa. 60:19.

Even the sun and moon shall become needless; in some new and more direct experience of God, they shall need nothing to reflect His light, but drink immediately from Himself His strength and inspiration. This is the meaning of the life of sacrifice; it has ever before it a positive rather than a negative end, and it aims at life, not death—death only as the gateway to a better life. It looks with no puritan eye of contempt at the fair things that the world has, or at those whose lives are less stern; it only gives up what it surrenders to gain something better.

For the power to give up many things—every earthly thing—is at bottom a power of not being able to do without other things. He to whom honor is necessary can do without money. He who must have goodness can get along without praise. He who must have God's communion can do without the sweet companionship of fellow men. He who cannot lose his eternity can easily cast aside time and the body that belongs to time, and by the martyr's slow or sudden death exchange the visible for the invisible, the symbol for the reality; nay, he who values most intensely his friend's or his child's life, can, not easily, but still not grudgingly, let go the joy and daily comfort of his friend's or his child's hourly presence, and see him die that he may enter into life.

On these two ladders, as it were, by these two seals, the order of human character mounts up—the power to do without and the power not to do without. As you grow better, there are some things that are always growing looser in their grasp upon you; there are other things that are always taking tighter hold upon your life. You sweep up out of the grasp of money, praise, ease, distinction. You sweep up into the necessity of truth, courage, virtue, love, and God. The gravitation of the earth grows weaker; the gravitation of the stars takes stronger and stronger hold upon you.

And, on the other hand, as you grow worse, as you go down the terrible opposite of all, this comes to pass. The highest necessities let you go and the lowest necessities take tighter hold of you.

Still, as you go down, you are judged by what you can do without and what you cannot do without. You come down at last where you cannot do without a comfortable dinner and an easy bed, but you can do without an act of charity or a thought of God. The poor sot finds his misery sealed with this double seal, that he cannot miss his glass of liquor and he can miss without a sigh every good company and virtuous wish.

The abiding in Christ, then, demands a surrender of all that hinders the union of the soul with Him. There is no broad rule that can be laid down beforehand; it is an individual matter between each soul and Christ. All possibility of pride or harsh criticism of others is out of the question, for none can judge beforehand of what another ought to give up. Each must follow as he is led, resolving that if need be he will give up all for all.

Let your mind be filled with the thought of Christ.
But again, the abiding in Christ involves the positive clinging to Him. It is like the growth of a friendship: at first these two people were very little to one another, but by familiarity and acts of kindness they got to know one another better. Then one took more hold upon the thoughts of the other, the influence became stronger, and when outwardly separated they were less and less apart in thought. Every faculty of the soul was brought under the influence of imagination, memory, and affection.

So it is with the soul's abiding in Christ; there is an ever-growing intimacy and interchange of thought; the mind is more constantly filled with His presence; His influence gradually penetrates through the whole soul, shaping and forming the character. The first question in coming to any decision is, "What would He wish?" The last question when any work is done is, "Will it be pleasing to Him?" The whole character is swayed and controlled by His influence. How wonderful it is to see many a rough, undisciplined self-centered man pass beneath the spell of that sacred presence and gradually become transformed: still, indeed, himself, but all with that unmistakable characteristic that betokens His work.

> For good ye are and bad, and like to coins,
> Some true, some light, but every one of you
> Stamped with the image of the King.[79]

If, then, the soul is abiding in Christ, the mind will be more and more filled with the thought of Him; His influence will be consciously felt in all one does. None can live near Him without becoming like Him.

Bear fruit through your union with Christ.
And, once more, the abiding in Christ is not all our own doing. If we are striving to hold fast to Him, we must remember that He is holding us more tightly still in His grasp. We often feel how difficult it is to keep near Him; but have we not felt, too, at times how difficult it is to break away from Him? He will not let us go. There have been times when inwardly we had altogether broken with Him, but He still kept His hand upon us and drew us back. We have sometimes rebelled at His persistence and felt, "I wish He would leave me to go my own way."

[79] Alfred Lord Tennyson, *Idylls of the King,* "The Holy Grail," lines 25ff.

No, it is not so easy to get free from His grasp; if ever there is a final breach between the soul and Christ, the last hand to loose its hold is His, not ours.

Now, the result of this life of union with Christ is that it brings forth fruit. "As the branch cannot bear fruit of itself, except it abide in the vine, no more can ye, except ye abide in me."[80] The branch is to be adorned with the fruit of the vine. "I am the vine, ye are the branches. He that abideth in me and I in him, the same bringeth forth much fruit, for apart from me ye can do nothing."[81] The soul is to be adorned with the graces of Christ; it is to show forth virtues that are not its own by nature, but are the result of the action of our Lord's life upon it.

As the sap of the vine circulates through the branch, so is the life of Christ to flow into and to nourish the soul, and this will have visible results: the branch will be laden with the fruit of the vine; it is unmistakable: "Of thorns men do not gather figs, nor of a bramble bush gather they grapes";[82] the fruit of the soul will betoken its union with the true vine. This is the purpose of all God's dealings with it, that it may bring forth not leaves only but fruit.

And for this purpose He prunes it. If it were not for the pruning, much of the sap would be exhausted in bringing forth leaves; but the husbandman prunes it, cutting off much of the over-luxuriant growth, that in the autumn there may be a plenteous harvest of fruit. The result of the pruning is at first a loss of the natural rich and undisciplined growth. The tree has lost under the pruning knife all its beauty, much of its apparent life, but

[80] John 15:4.
[81] John 15:5.
[82] Luke 6:44.

time shows that the husbandman acted wisely when the grapes begin to fill and ripen.

Now our Lord says, "I am the true vine and my Father is the husbandman."[83] His cause and ours is the same. He is the vine, we the branches; therefore, the Father deals with every branch with the same tender care He has for the vine. To injure the branch is to injure the tree; we are sure while we abide in the vine that no real harm shall happen unto us, although much that is beautiful and the outcome of the free play of life may need to be pruned away, and although we cannot see the wisdom of much that is done until long after, until the time of the ripening fruit comes.

But all this most people can understand. We all know how much we need to be dealt with and disciplined by one who understands us better than we know ourselves and whose love is strong enough to take from us those harmful things that we have not the courage to give up ourselves.

If only we can perceive the action of the Husbandman, we are prepared to accept it humbly and patiently.

But how many things happen that it seems impossible to trace to the hand of God—nay, that we can clearly trace to a very different hand, the hand not of love but of hate. How often have the sins of another been the discipline of one's life, sometimes with a refinement of cruelty that seems diabolical. Two persons are bound together in marriage, seemingly to curse and ruin one another. A husband takes pleasure in hurting his wife in every possible way, in throwing every difficulty in her path when she tries to do right, seeking to degrade her and rob her of all self-respect; or a wife makes her husband's life unbearable.

[83] John 15:1.

How is it possible to attribute such things to God? Many a person says, "If I could see God's hand in all this, I would try to accept it, but I cannot."

But we must distinguish between the pruning knife and the hand that holds it. There need be neither wisdom nor love in the knife. It cannot even cut unless someone takes it into his hand. The gardener takes that steel and directs and controls it. By itself, it cannot lop off any leaf or any branch; it can only do the work that it is directed to do.

No, there is no love in the blade itself, but along its sharp edge there trembles the love and the wisdom of the gardener who uses it. "Thou couldst have no power at all against me except it were given thee from above."[84] So said our Lord to Pilate, whose cowardice and weakness were, as it were, His pruning knife.

He looked not at the knife, but at the hand that held it: "My Father is the husbandman."

If we try to do this, we shall often see the wisdom and the love that directs and controls the most ruthless cruelty of another in its action upon our life. Her love for her worthless son may have been the scourge of a woman's life; yes, and as we look deeper, we can see it was to all human appearance the only thing that could have brought her to God. The knife was wisely guided, even though it cut so deep. That fair home was wrecked by that woman's sin, and her husband was so proud of his home, and loved it so; it was perhaps just the one point on which he could be reached. While the things of earth were so happy, he had no thought for the deeper things of life, and the knife cut it all cruelly away, and then in time the fruit began to appear, although

[84] John 19:11.

for a long time that life looked unshapely and bare, and almost without the power to put itself forth again.

It will be always so: the Husbandman can use any knife, but He will always act with wisdom and with love. For the pruning is a token that the branch has the possibility of bearing fruit: "Every branch that beareth fruit He pruneth it, that it may bring forth more fruit."[85]

Therefore, if the soul has come to Christ and is abiding in Him, it must expect to find the hand of God upon it. In all that comes upon it, it must look beyond the mere instrument through which its troubles immediately come; it must look to see the hand that holds and guides the knife, and it must yield itself to the discipline, only longing that its life may be enriched and adorned by the fruit that comes from the branches abiding in the vine.

[85] Cf. John 15:2.

Chapter 10

⁓

Persevere

There are virtues that are of so strong and independent a nature that they seem able to stand alone and to live on when everything else in the soul that is noble has died. One sometimes meets people who are corrupt to the heart's core and yet are not wanting in generosity — that one remnant of better days endures while everything else is gone. Or again, there are people who, while they have lost all the virtues that belong to the gentler side of their nature, and have become hard and bitter and censorious, yet have a very strong and masterful sense of duty. But as we get to know these people better, we shall find that while the form of the virtue remains, the substance is practically gone, although, so far as it goes, it is good; but it is rather of nature than of grace. The spendthrift generosity of the prodigal is a very different thing from the Christian grace of charity; still it is, so far as it goes, a virtue, and it is often a surprise and a joy to find how long some such virtues will live on amidst the corruption and evil around them.

Then, too, there are virtues that never stand alone. They are of so delicate a texture that they need some other virtue to protect them and upon which they may rest. Purity will nearly always grow, resting upon the prop of humility. Let humility fail, and purity, like some fading flower, will begin to bend earthward and to lose its bloom. Inward peace twines itself around the strong support of self-oblation. Even moral courage that seems so strong and self-reliant will gain strength and a firmer root in the soul if it grows upon the tender yet unbending support of penitence. Let penitence deepen, and moral courage will grow so strong that one who is naturally weak will be ready to face every difficulty and danger; let penitence begin to die, and the will that was so strong and brave becomes cowardly.

Thus, there are virtues that are like twin sisters and always grow in pairs, the virtue that seems the more robust often depending for its life on one that appears far more delicate. They grow in pairs, and they die in pairs. When one begins to droop, the other is sure to droop with it; it cannot stand alone. Self-forgetfulness depends on the practice of the presence of God. When the soul has gained this hidden grace, it will show in its outer life that other virtue that everyone must see and admire, yet none can tell on what a very delicate and hidden support it depends for its extraordinary strength. Let the presence of God grow dim within and the presence of self at once presses to the front.

Thus, it often happens that the virtue that we most need and desire is not to be cultivated directly, but through some other virtue that at first sight may seem to have little connection with it, yet as we watch it growing we shall generally find that the other virtue has twined itself round it, or followed close upon it.

We scarcely realize how purity is very often best gained, not by a direct struggle for it, but by striving for humility; and as humility grows we shall surely find that it has brought with it the grace of purity, how or why we may not be able to tell.

Persevere

It is impossible to fight directly against self-consciousness. The effort to rid oneself of it by watching against it only roots it more deeply; but as we strive directly to practice the presence of God, we find it has brought with it its twin sister that will not come without it, and the consciousness of self has melted away in the light of God's presence.

Again, many vices spring from virtues unbalanced by some other virtue that develops the opposite side of the character. One may, for instance, be all heart and no head, or all head and no heart. If so, the powers, great and noble as they are, that belong to heart or head will fail of producing their proper fruit, for they are unbalanced and one-sided. There are virtues that belong to one side of the character and leave the other untouched, and consequently each needs the other to balance and correct it. All prayer and no action, except in the case of very exceptional vocations, may lead to great self-deceit. All action and no prayer fritters away the powers of the soul.

Thus, the virtues that belong to one side of the character need those on the other side to balance them, or they cease to be virtues. Consequently, the Christian life is always a surprise, for it is ever showing seemingly opposite characteristics. But it will also display what is more beautiful still, single virtues that are the outcome of the perfect blending of two graces that are seemingly in opposition. The new virtue is the result of these two being blended in perfect proportion; let the proportion be destroyed, and the virtue itself is destroyed.

The virtue of Christian patience is the outcome of the perfect blending of gentleness and strength; if these two do not mingle in perfect proportion, it ceases to be patience. If gentleness outweighs strength, patience degenerates into weakness; if strength outweighs gentleness, it crystallizes into hardness. Firmness is the blending in perfect proportion of strength of will and clearness of moral judgment; if there be not the latter, or in proportion as it is lacking, firmness will degenerate into obstinacy or scrupulosity; if strength of will be not in due proportion, then it is not firmness at all, but passes off into insincerity or even hypocrisy.

But once more, there are virtues that are more comprehensive in their character. They are the condition and support of every other virtue; there are certain Christian graces that, without which, you can have none, and, with which, all others become possible. They represent attitudes of the soul that fit it for the growth of virtue in general.

There are two such especially, without which no one can mature in any Christian grace. One is, as it were, the soil out of which all must grow—charity. Any virtue that has not spread its roots into this, and that does not suck its nourishment from it, is not a Christian grace. "Though I have the gift of prophecy, and understand all mysteries and all knowledge; and though I have all faith, so that I could remove mountains, and have not charity, I am nothing; and though I bestow all my goods to feed the poor, and though I give my body to be burned, and have not charity, it profiteth me nothing."[86] Charity is the soil in which alone Christian virtues can grow. It is the condition of all else. Although it seems the end, it is the beginning, for there is no virtue where it is not.

And there is another, without which no virtue can mature its growth. Perseverance is not merely the crown and stamp of perfection; it must accompany every step in the growth of every grace. Just as the texture of the tree must be woven firm in every stage of its growth, so perseverance has to watch over the growth

[86] 1 Cor. 13:2–3.

of each virtue day by day. Every day in which it fails, the graces that are under its care begin to droop and lose their bloom.

Thus, perseverance is not only a virtue in itself, but it is one without whose constant presence and assistance no other virtue can develop one step in its growth. If charity, then, be the soil into which all must spread their roots, perseverance is the cohesive force that gives form and consistency to all over whose development it presides. And thus, temptation will often leave unassailed all the graces that the soul is trying to form and attack the one grace of perseverance; for it knows well that if it can destroy or weaken this, all else must fail with it.

We often meet people with very high aspirations and the beginnings of many graces and with great possibilities, but nothing in them matures, nothing attains its full bloom, for they are lacking in the one grace that is the guardian and protector of all — they have no perseverance.

Now, perseverance having so great a work to do, having to watch over every good thing that the soul would develop, cannot work alone — it has not only to keep everything under its protection, but it must live in both the present and the future; it must look forward, but it must not for a moment forget the present. It knows indeed that many a promising virtue has died because its possessor was living in the future and neglecting it in the present, and virtues are too delicate to grow untended for even a day. And it knows also that many a virtue has been killed because the soul in which it was trying to grow could not, when it saw the blade, look forward and wait and hope, recognizing the law of its organic growth and rejoicing in the thought of the full-grown ear.

Therefore, perseverance needs the aid of two fellow workers: it needs, as it were, eyes with which to look forward and hands with which to toil. It must keep ever before it the ideal toward which it presses, and it must never cease to work toward that ideal. Perseverance is not a mere dogged plodding on toward an unseen end; it is full of inspiration and enthusiasm. In all its endeavors, therefore, it is assisted by the two fellow workers, hope and patience.

Natural hope is the spring of all the movement of life, of all activity and progress. Memory links us with the past; hope looks forward. It is almost creative, as, aided by imagination, it lifts the veil from the future.

Men are ready to forgo the greatest enjoyments in the present in the desire of what hope promises, but if in the midst of their plans hope dies, then their hands fall heavily by their side. As we look at the busy world, with all its competitions and sacrifice, and ask what is the spring that sets it in motion, we answer, *hope*. The manifold powers of heart and mind and will are developed and unfolded under its inspiration.

And it is the same in the spiritual life.

Hope here receives a new direction; it looks to no earthly end; it looks to heaven. It stimulates men to no mere temporal activities but to the development of Christian graces and the preparation for the vision of God. It sees the end already attained, the prize won, and that vision, as it beams brighter and brighter, kindles the soul with ambitions so great that it is prepared, before it has obtained a single grace except this one, to forgo everything for this end.

Faith looks backward as well as forward; hope looks only forward. Faith embraces in its vision heaven and hell; hope cannot see hell; it cannot contemplate failure. It sees what it aims for as already its possession and then gathers all its forces to succeed.

Thus, perseverance is aided and inspired by hope. And patience, the unwearied worker, plods on enlightened and sustained by hope, never resting, never fainting. While the eyes of hope are resting on the far-off vision of attainment, the hands of patience work steadily on to accomplish its present task. So it was with Peter. Our Lord lifted the veil and showed him the future, his end, the martyr's death: "When thou shalt be old, thou shalt stretch forth thy hands, and another shall gird thee, and carry thee whither thou wouldest not. This said He, signifying what death he should glorify God."[87] That was what he was to work toward: "And when he had spoken this, he said unto him, Follow me."[88]

If that end was to be reached, he must now be following Christ; he must work for it in the present.

Thus that workaday, commonplace virtue, perseverance, is full of inspiration. Hope the idealist and patience the practical plodder cooperate to accomplish her task. As days and years go by and she goes on steadily and unswervingly with her work, it is not all mere dry, hard plodding. Bright dreams burn before her eyes and kindle her heart; she is all on fire within, even though she looks so calm and commonplace, for hope ever stands by her side like a prophet to stimulate and inspire. She works like an artist with the model before her eyes and the chisel and hammer in her hands, and like an artist her heart burns within her as she works.

Perseverance, therefore, may fail in one of two ways: either by losing hope or by losing patience. If hope fails, the work will lose all life and inspiration and will become mechanical; if patience, it will never be completed.

Thus, some persons go on with their religious duties, their prayers and rule or whatever it may be they have undertaken,

[87] John 21:18.
[88] Cf. John 21:19.

but it can easily be seen after a time that there is no heart in what they are doing. It becomes more and more mechanical and lifeless; it does not develop or strengthen the character; it might as well be given up. Perhaps it would be better to give it up, for there is no effort to gain anything through what is being done. Hope has died. There is no looking forward to the end, and the hands work heavily.

Others, again, begin with enthusiasm, are borne along for a time by the strength of their enthusiastic impulse, but at the first failure they lose patience and give up. They see the end; the eye of hope is open and kindles the heart, but they cannot endure the failures and delays that come between the vision and its fulfillment. Sometimes they end in becoming mere dreamers, thinking what one day they will do, imagining themselves only held back by circumstances, living a life of dreams with their eyes fixed upon the far-off future and their hands fallen listlessly by their sides, forgetting that the only way to fulfill their hopes is by present effort. Thus, two different kinds of persons will fail of the grace of perseverance in quite different ways.

But how are such elements of failure to be corrected, for they apparently belong to the very character itself?

They can be corrected only through union with Christ. There is natural despondency and supernatural hope; natural impulsiveness and supernatural patience. It is necessary for many that they learn deeply through failure after failure that they have no power of themselves to help themselves before they can learn the meaning of these great words: "I can do all things through Christ who strengtheneth me."[89] He who said them had learned it, for

---

[89] Cf. Phil. 4:13.

he said again: "When I am weak, then am I strong."[90] He was conscious at the same time of natural weakness and supernatural strength. He had learned through his own incapacity where to find the power he needed.

There is no necessary connection between a naturally hopeful and bright disposition and the Christian grace of hope; it is not impossible that these may exist in inverse proportion in the same person. Natural hopefulness may not be able to survive constant failure in moral and spiritual things.

The despair that springs from the sense of one's weakness and the breaking down of resolution after resolution may be the birth pangs of Christian hope. Only when the soul has suffered much from many physicians and finds itself growing no better, but rather worse, does it at last come to our Lord. The constant sense of failure, the seeming powerlessness to stand before certain temptations, may be the means of leading one to find a new sense of power: "All my fresh springs shall be in thee."[91]

Consequently, the power of a sustained and unfailing hopefulness by which perseverance may be gained does not depend on—is, indeed, altogether independent of—natural disposition; it is based upon and grows out of spiritual experience. The soul has learned that in the moment of weakness, Christ can strengthen it; that, in spite of the most rooted habits, it can, in the power of our Lord, withstand old temptations before which once it was powerless. The hope that it has gained is built upon a surer foundation than any gift of nature; it is built upon the experienced truth of the promises of Christ.

[90] 2 Cor. 12:10.
[91] Cf. Ps. 87:7.

Thus, in the life of the soul that goes plodding on and struggling with its faults and temptations, there are often to be found two stages: first, failure and discouragement and a loss of interest or joy in what it is doing, and, not unfrequently, the sense of going through one's duties in a mechanical and lifeless way; and then there "springs up a light for the righteous, and joyful gladness for them who"—in spite of all failure—"are true of heart."[92] The heart is refreshed and the will invigorated as the eye stretches beyond the present and sees the accomplished end. Divine hope has come, and all is changed.

It is the same with patience: impulse wears away, and things undertaken in the excitement of some strong emotion are left unfinished. The experience of life teaches the soul that the noblest dreams and the highest ideals will not be fulfilled by fitful efforts, however strong and passionate they may be while they last, and that great ambitions do not of themselves make one great. At last it learns that what it needs is the disciplined faithfulness, sustained by rule and principle amidst all the fluctuations of feeling.

This it gains in Christ. All the bright dreams of what it hoped to be fade and form anew around another center, our Lord Himself; and as the soul tries to approach that center, it finds that it cannot by impulsive efforts, but only by constant and growing habits of mind and action.

It learns that in an hour's reaction after some time of spiritual excitement, it may lose more than it gained. It learns that they who would know Christ must be strong and patient and live on through times of coldness and apparent rejection.

[92] Cf. Ps. 97:11.

Thus, it learns the lesson of patience and discipline at the feet of Christ, and as it does, it sees, too, how its ideal becomes transformed, and with hopeful patience it fights its way on to its final triumph in Him.

Do we not know such men, who go on quietly and steadily fighting their way through difficulty after difficulty, never giving in to the sense of failure that would bid them give up, and never losing sight of their end; who, under the inspiration of hope, are protected from becoming mechanical, and under the protection of patience are preserved from the discouragements that beset the pathway of progress, and thus, beneath the guardianship of perseverance enrich their souls with many virtues that mature and ripen to perfection?

Biographical Note

Basil W. Maturin (1847–1915) was born in Ireland and educated at Trinity College in Dublin. First ordained as an Anglican priest, he was sent to Philadelphia in 1876, where he served as pastor of St. Clement's Church.

In 1897, at the age of fifty-one, he converted to Roman Catholicism and was ordained a Catholic priest the following year.

Both before and after his conversion, Fr. Maturin was famous for his preaching and psychological insight: he had a profound gift for guiding souls.

In 1913 he was appointed Catholic chaplain to the University of Oxford. In 1915, at the age of sixty-eight, he made a successful preaching tour of the United States, booking return passage on the RMS *Lusitania*. He was on board the *Lusitania* when a German U-boat torpedoed the ship. Fr. Maturin drowned after helping numerous other passengers to safety.

Sophia Institute

Sophia Institute is a nonprofit institution that seeks to nurture the spiritual, moral, and cultural life of souls and to spread the Gospel of Christ in conformity with the authentic teachings of the Roman Catholic Church.

Sophia Institute Press fulfills this mission by offering translations, reprints, and new publications that afford readers a rich source of the enduring wisdom of mankind.

Sophia Institute also operates two popular online Catholic resources: CrisisMagazine.com and CatholicExchange.com.

Crisis Magazine provides insightful cultural analysis that arms readers with the arguments necessary for navigating the ideological and theological minefields of the day. *Catholic Exchange* provides world news from a Catholic perspective as well as daily devotionals and articles that will help you to grow in holiness and live a life consistent with the teachings of the Church.

In 2013, Sophia Institute launched Sophia Institute for Teachers to renew and rebuild Catholic culture through service to Catholic education. With the goal of nurturing the spiritual, moral, and cultural life of souls, and an abiding respect for the role and work of teachers, we strive to provide materials and programs that are at once enlightening to the mind and ennobling to the heart; faithful and complete, as well as useful and practical.

Sophia Institute gratefully recognizes the Solidarity Association for preserving and encouraging the growth of our apostolate over the course of many years. Without their generous and timely support, this book would not be in your hands.

www.SophiaInstitute.com
www.CatholicExchange.com
www.CrisisMagazine.com
www.SophiaInstituteforTeachers.org